creativity

against

the world

Villa Vuoto Publications
Copyright © 2002 - 2005

ISBN: 1 519792 89 1
EAN-13: 978 1 519792 89 1
Expanded Edition
438
470

Text and illustrations by
Matthew Schlueb

for
Silly Sake

origin of creativity:

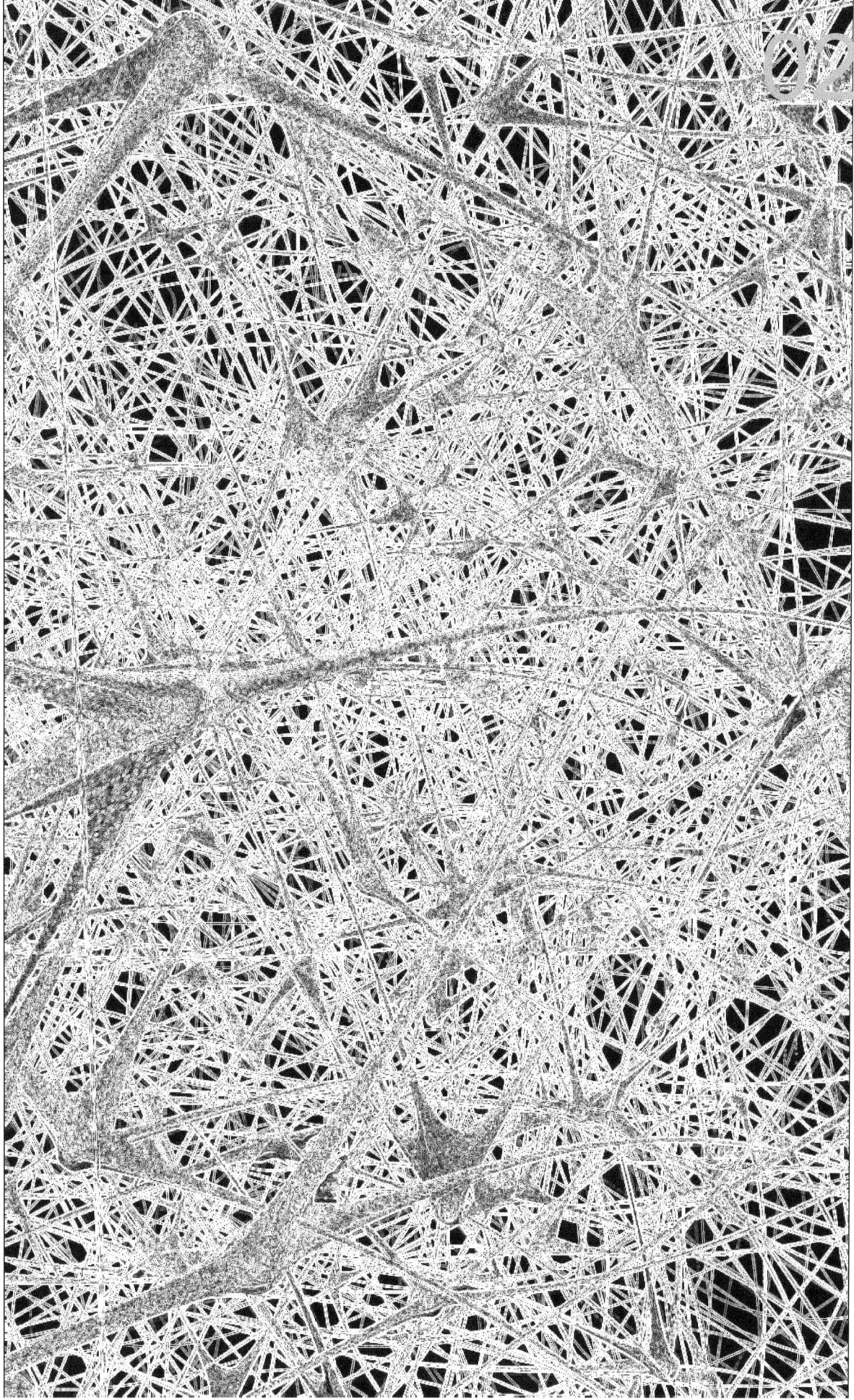
023

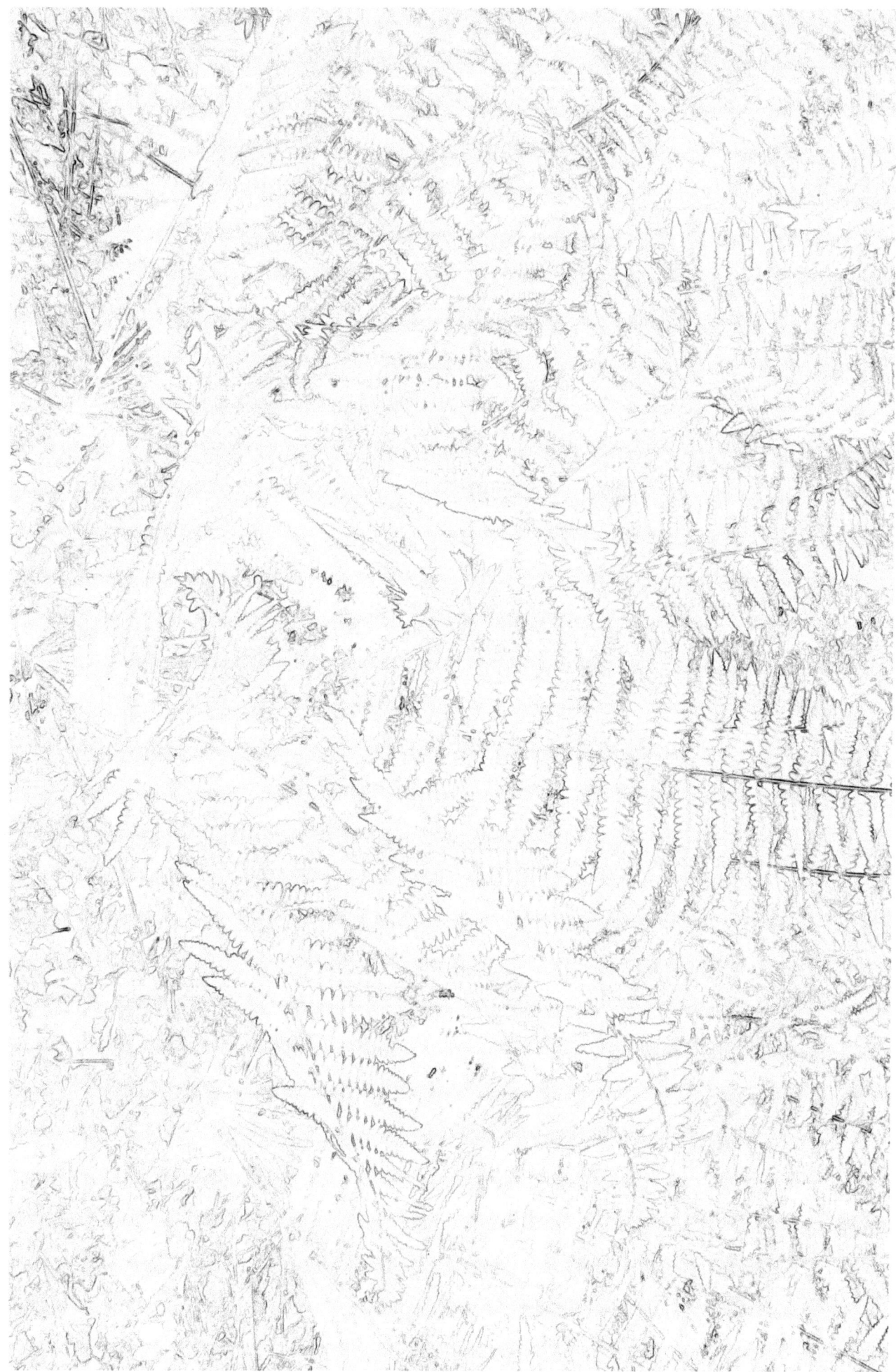

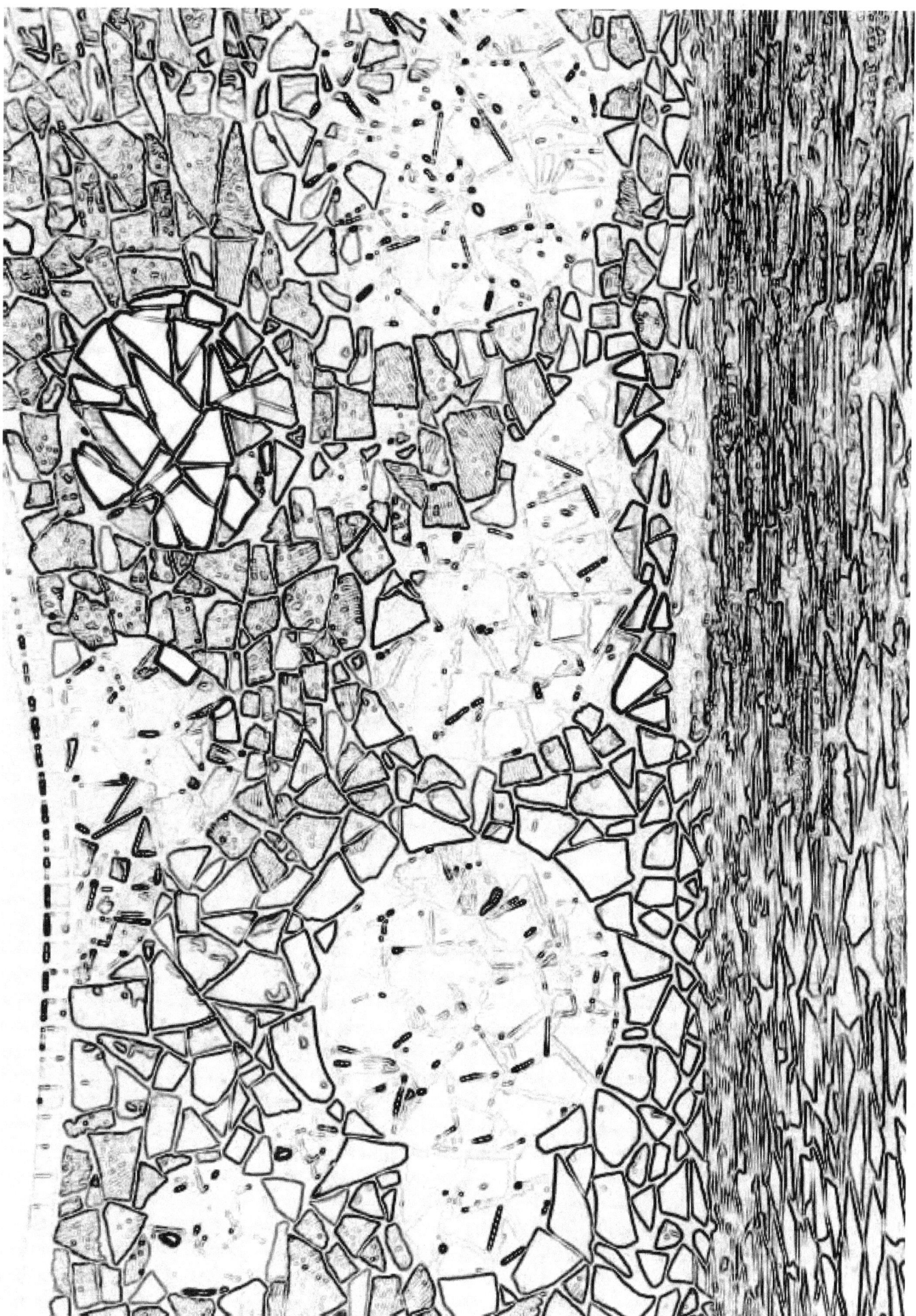

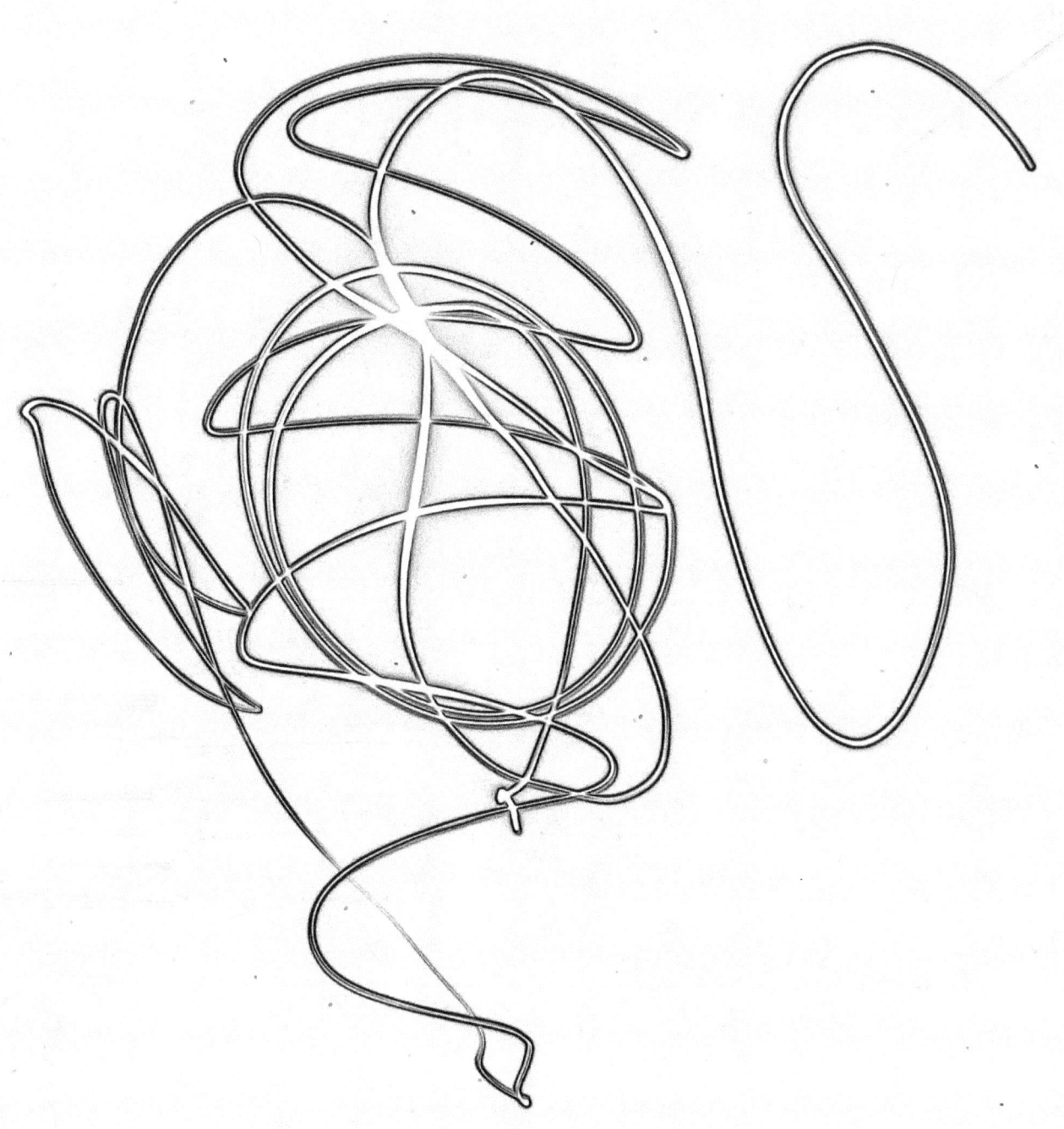

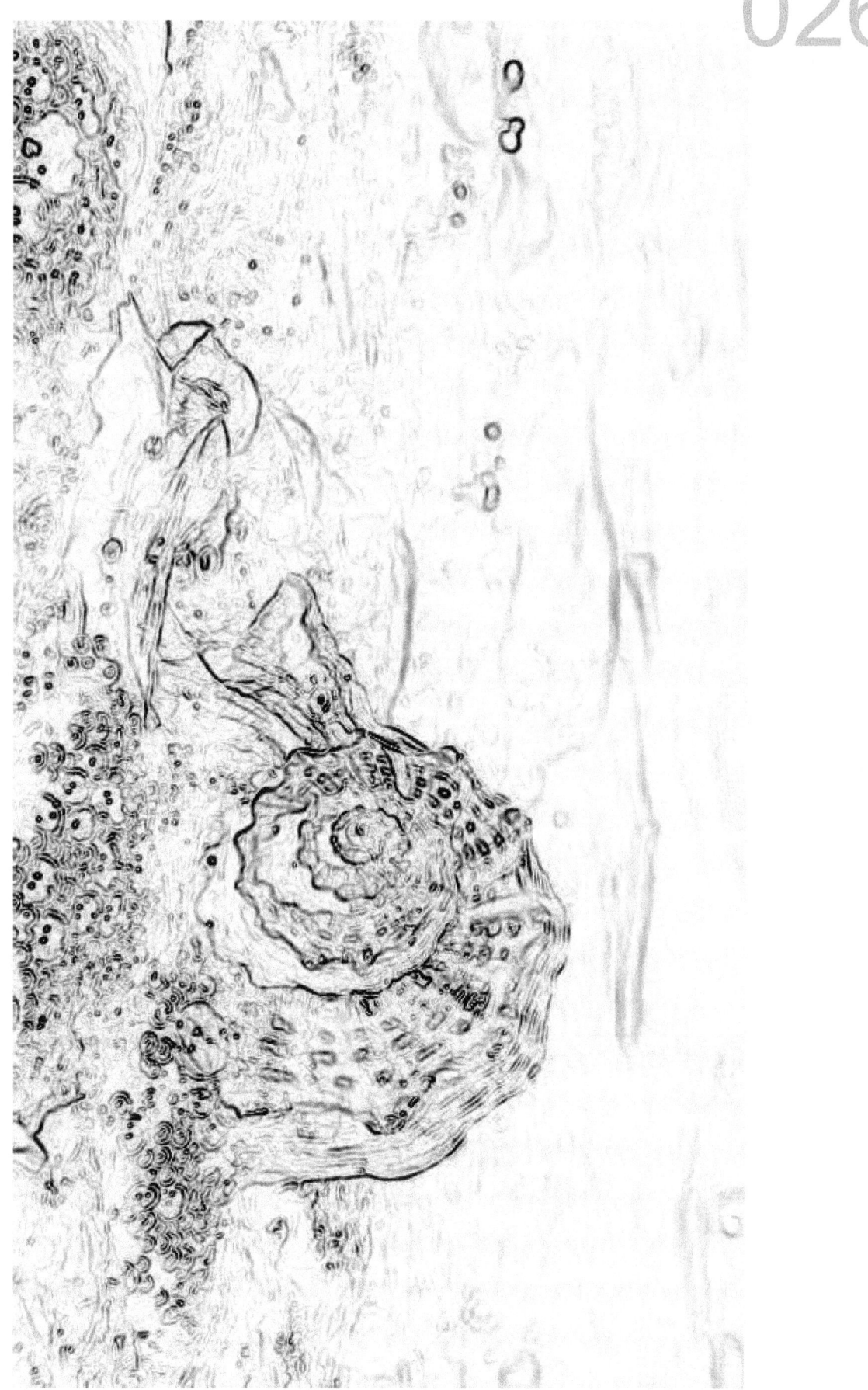

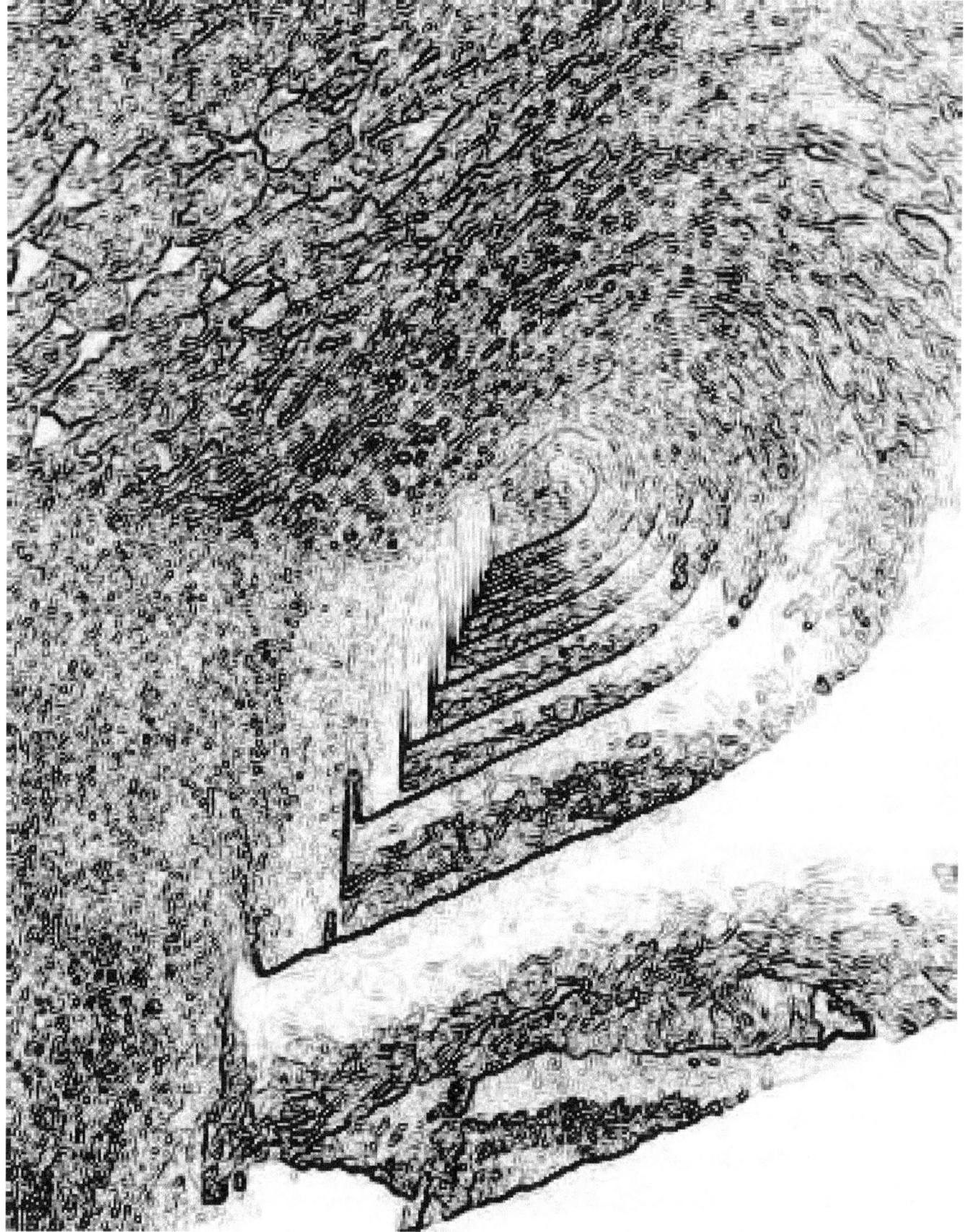

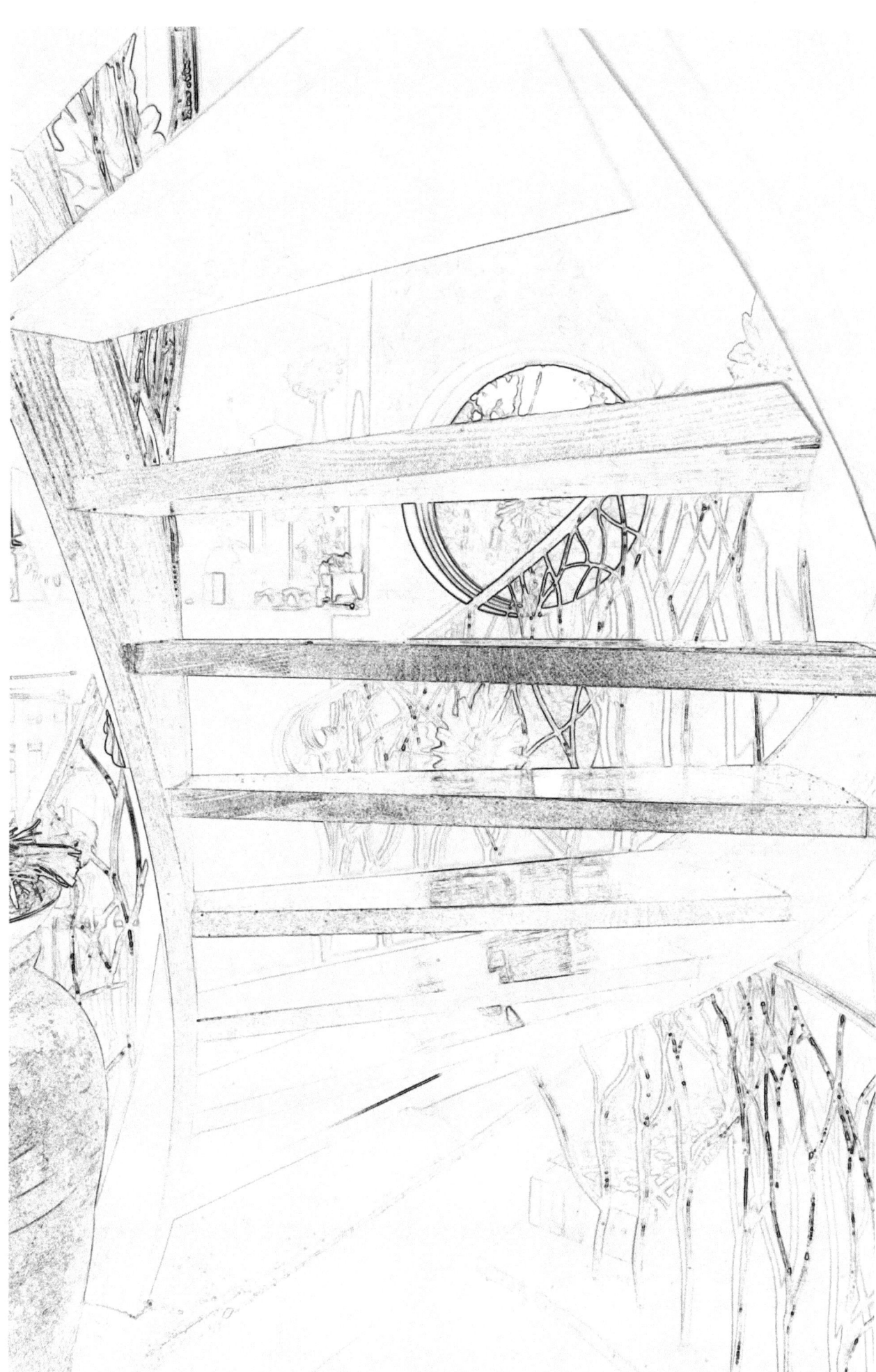

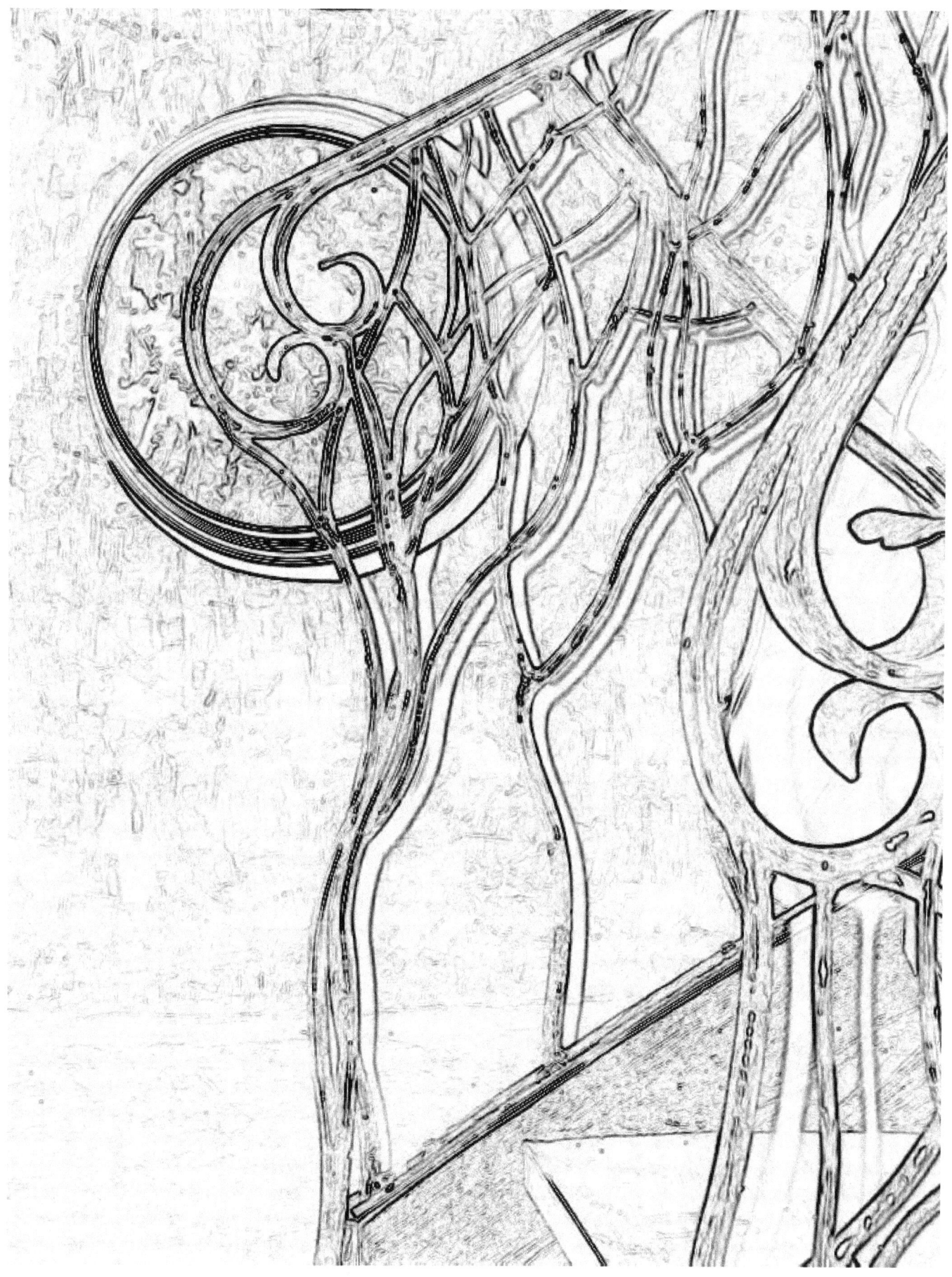

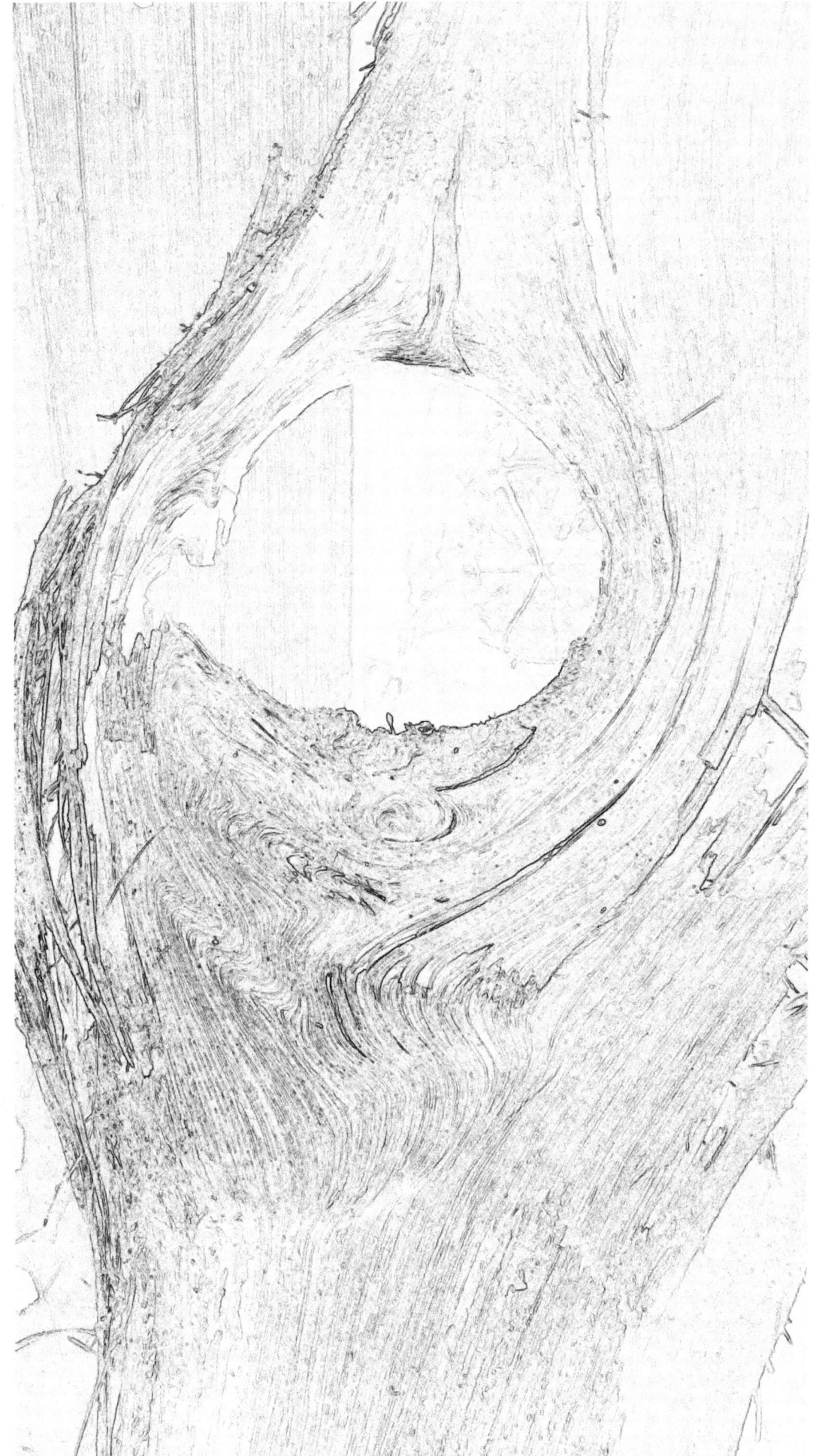

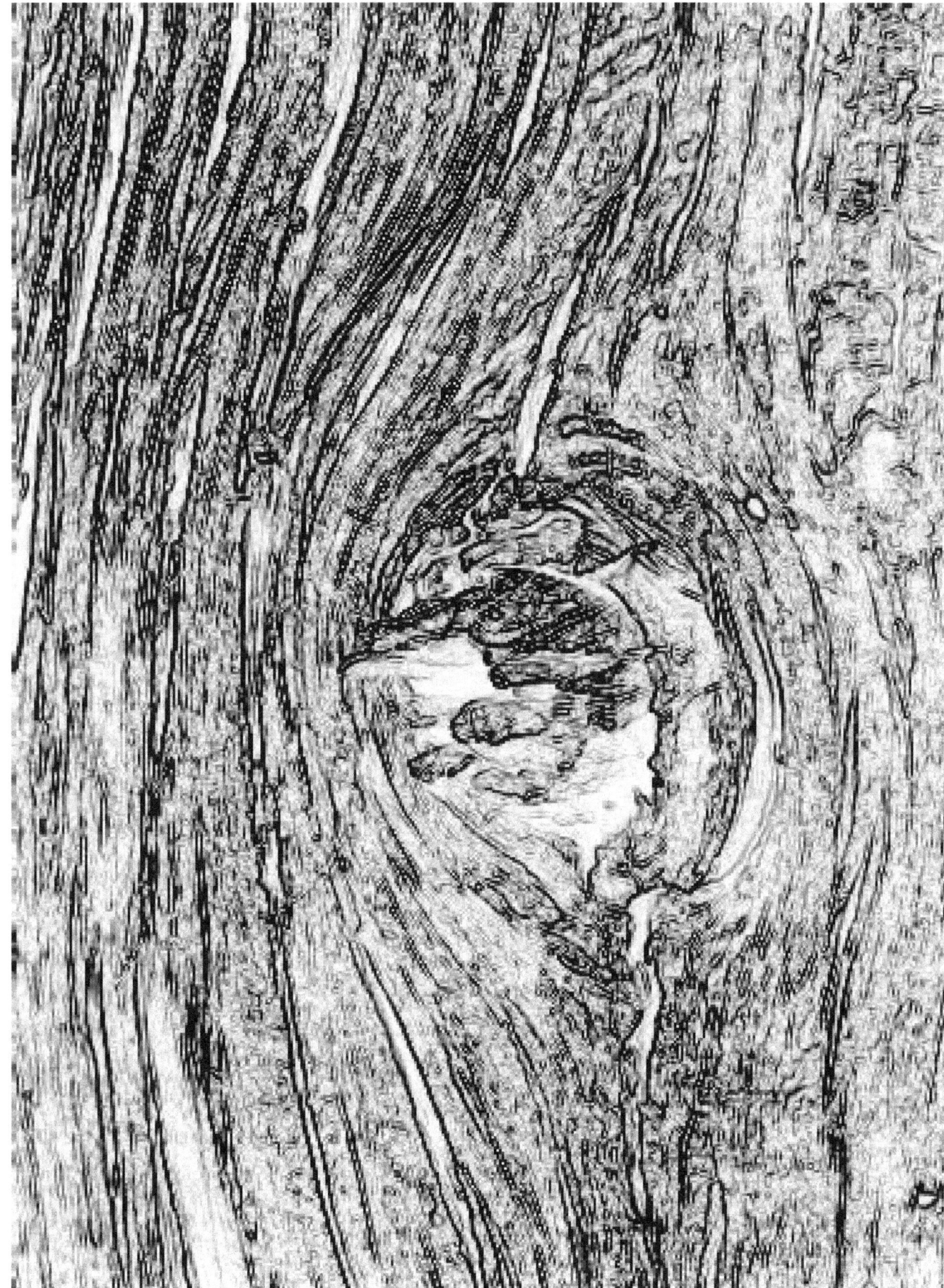

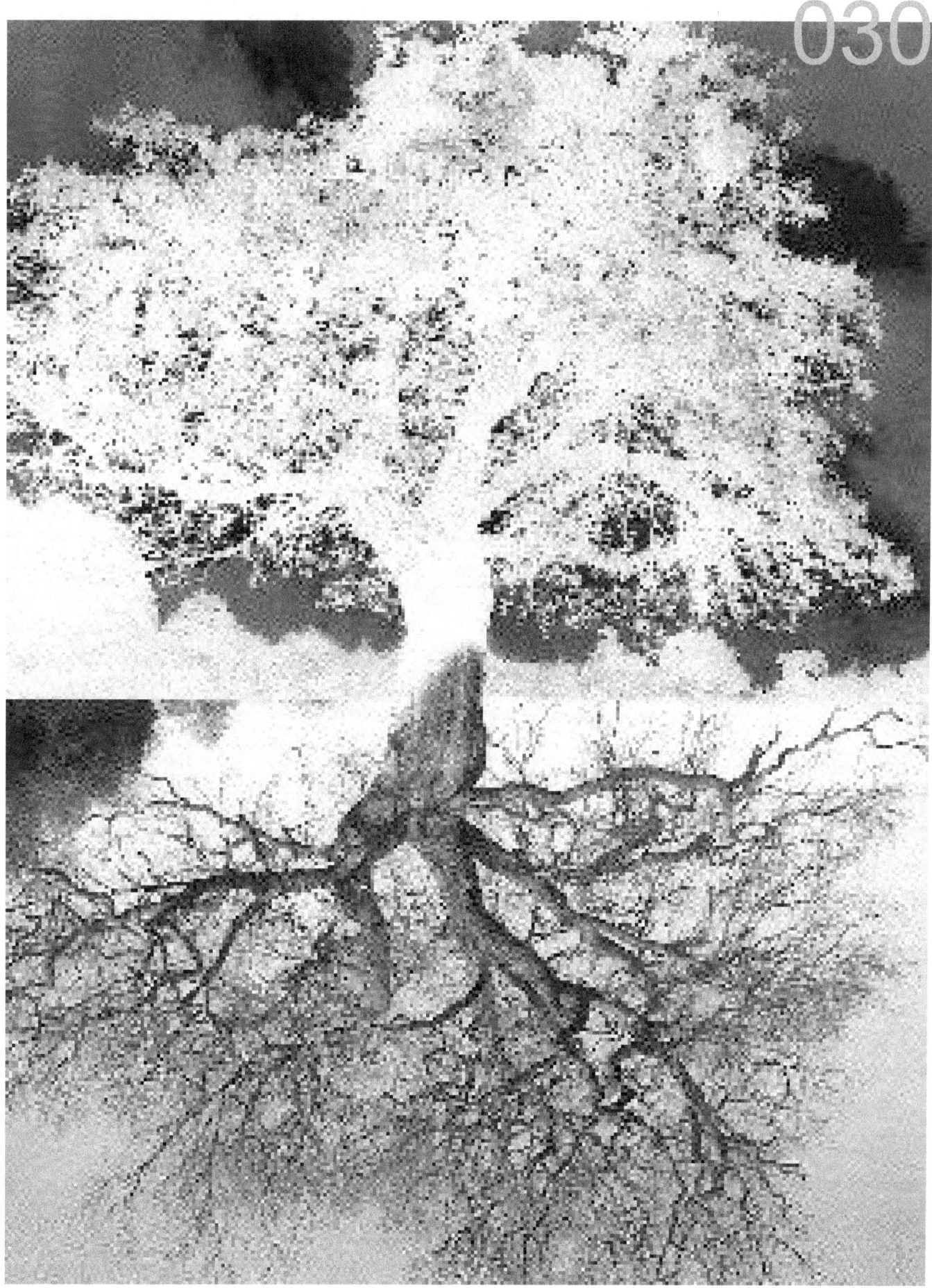

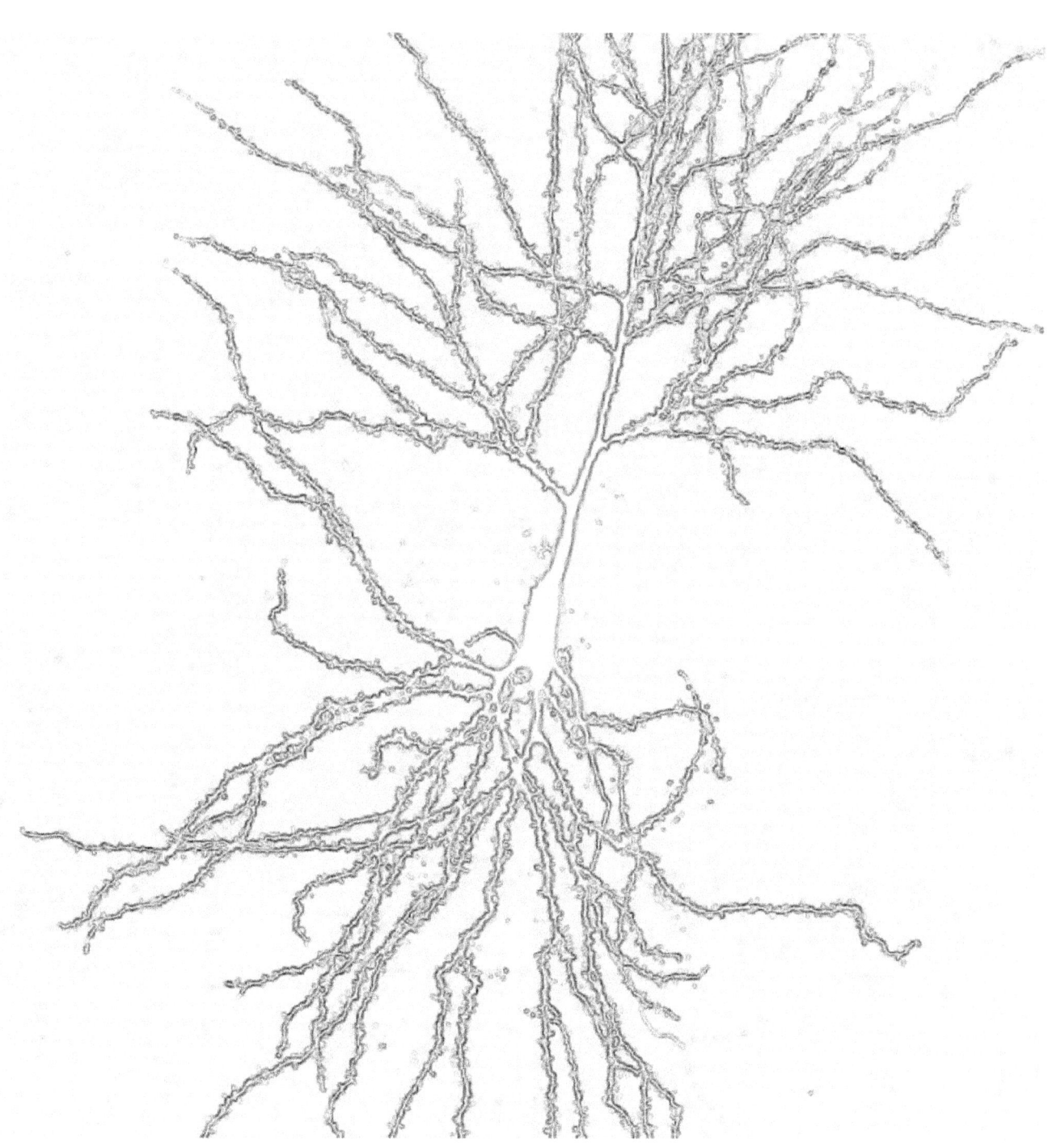

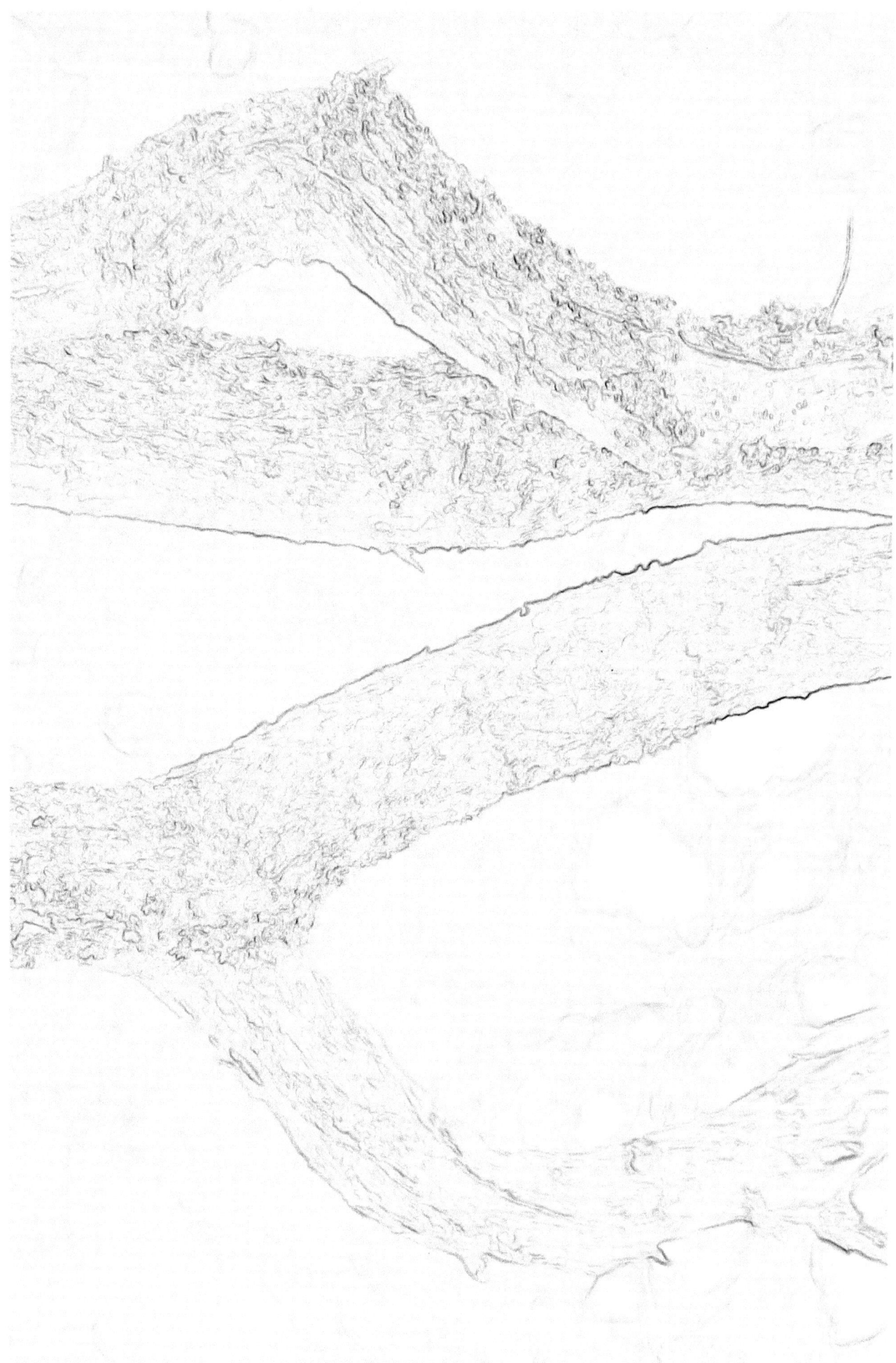

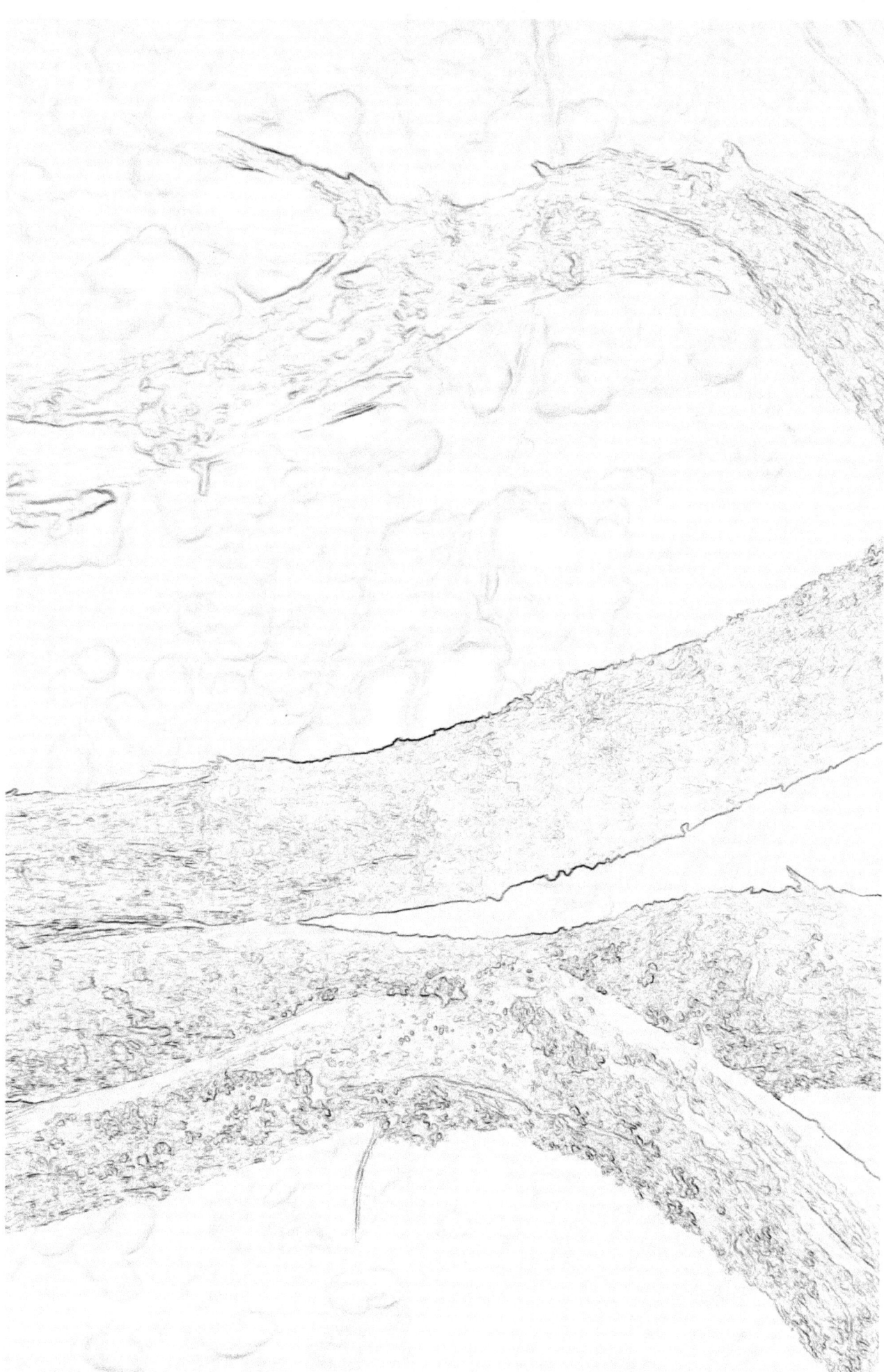

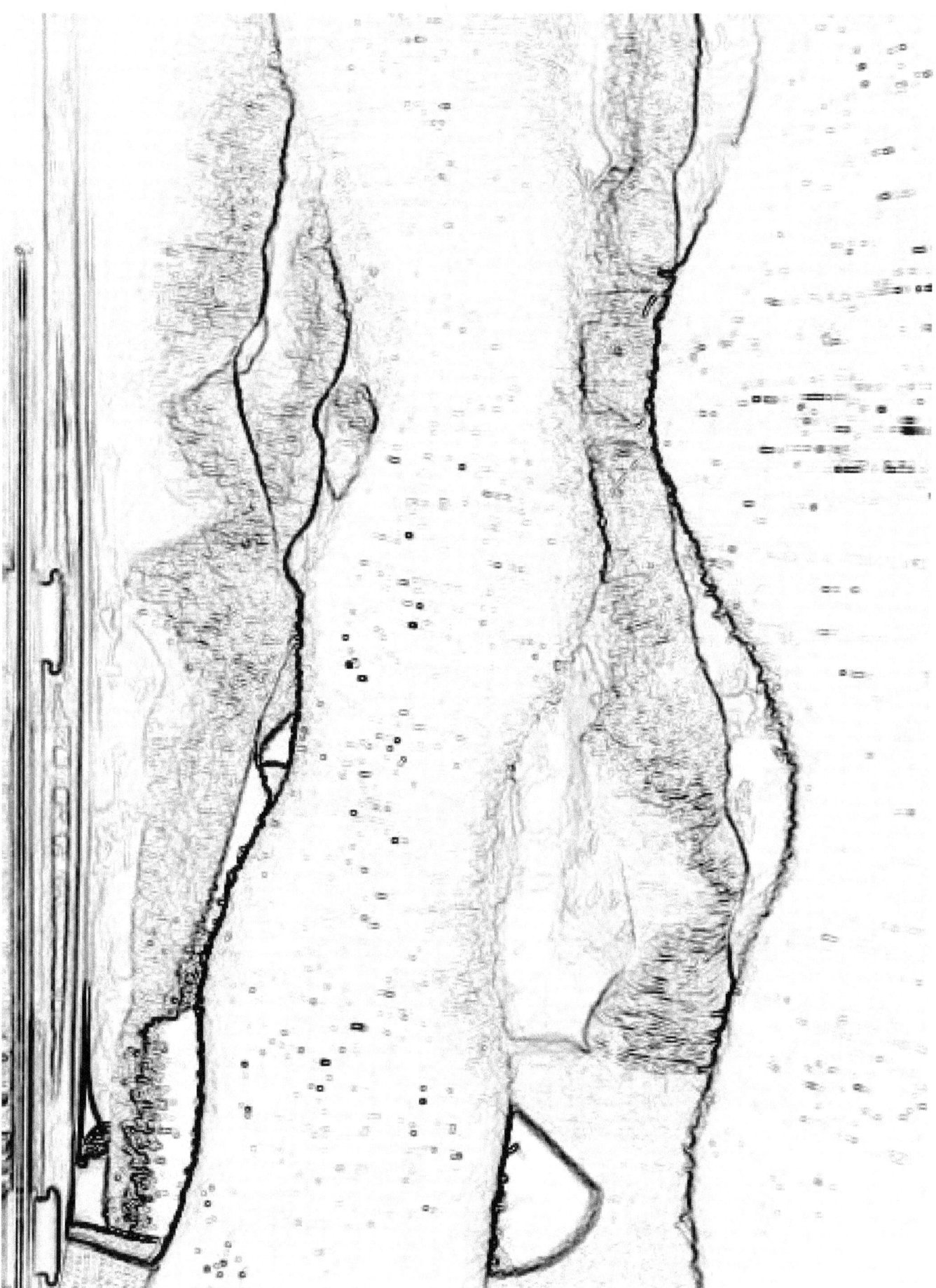

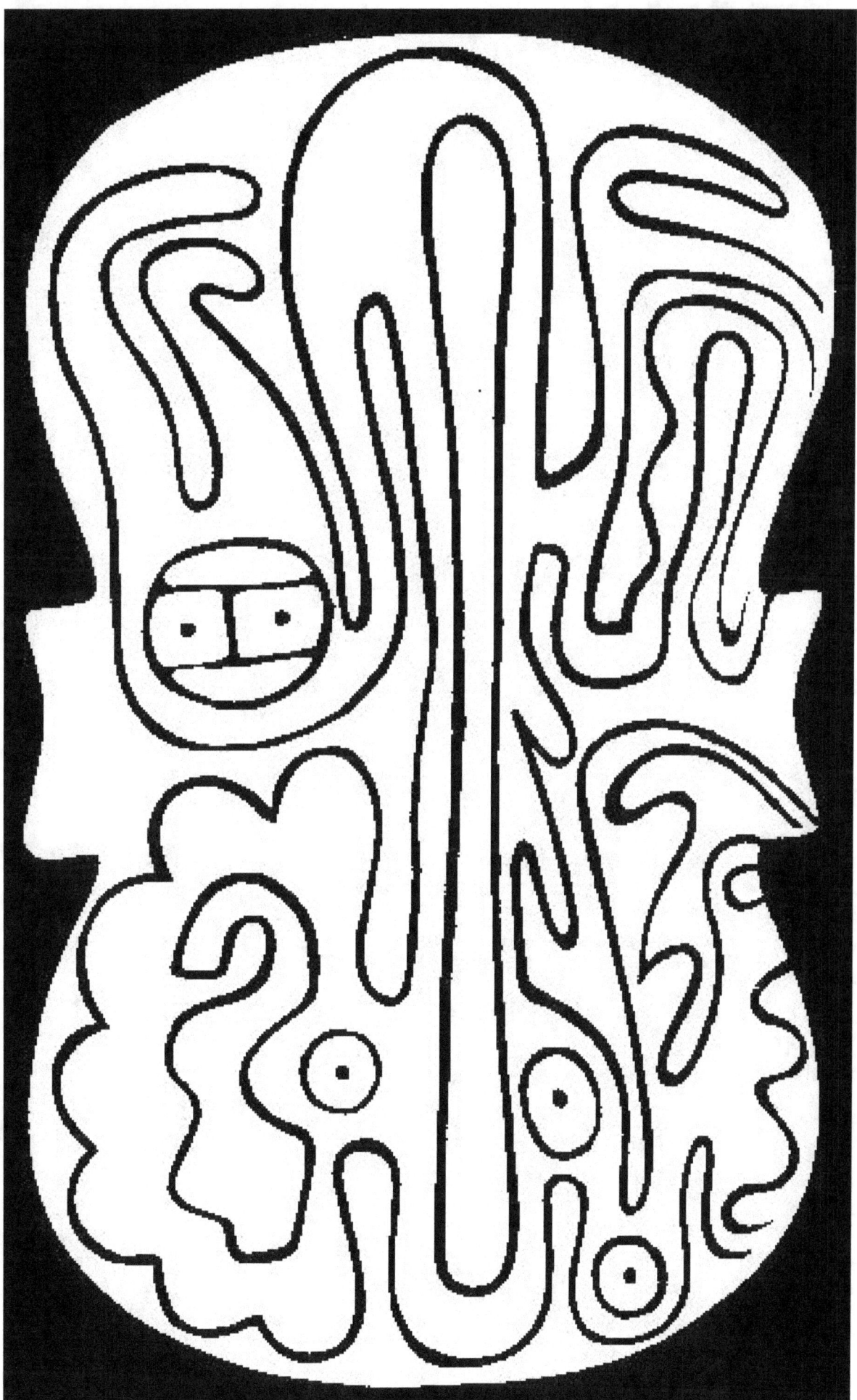

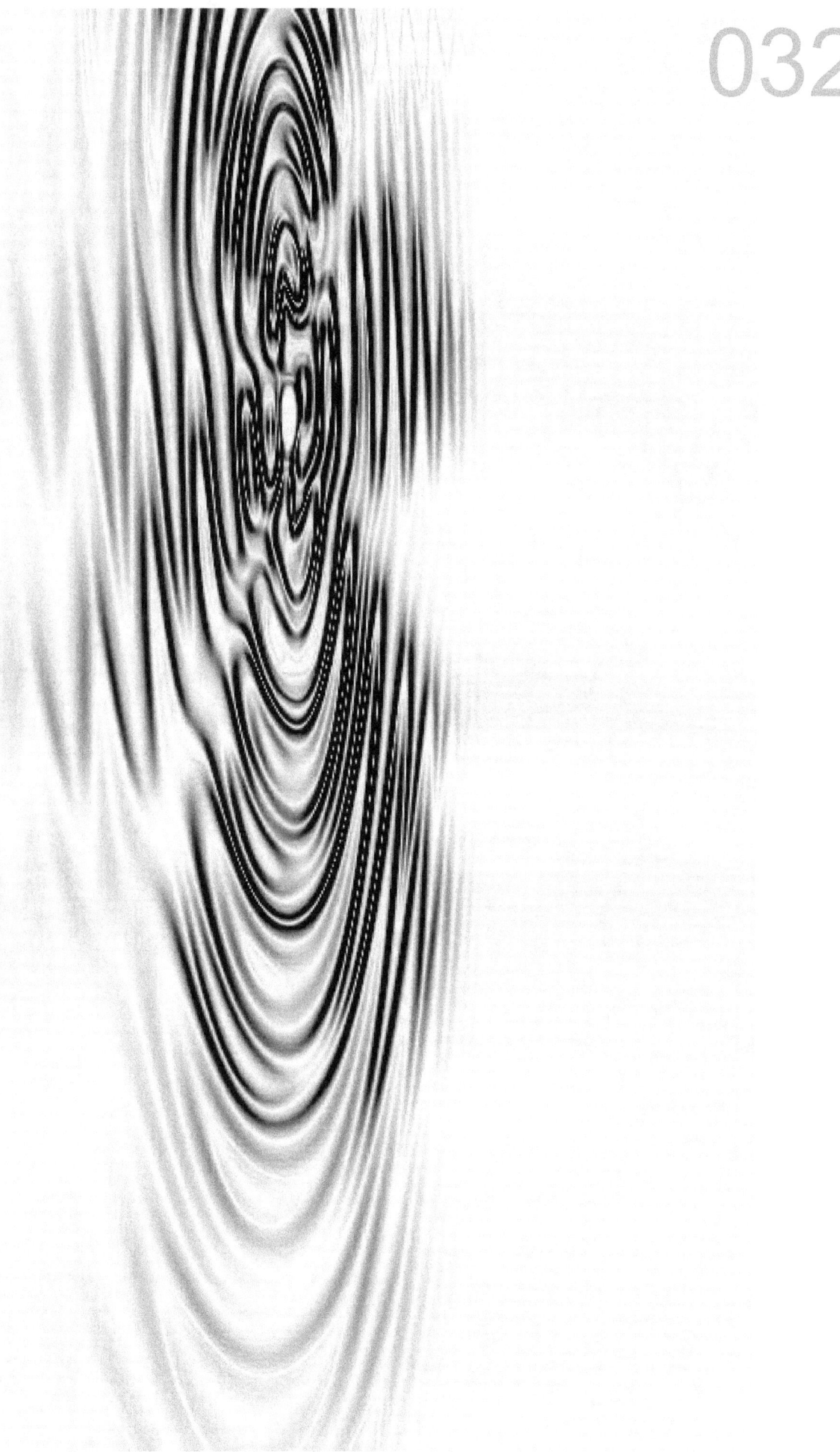

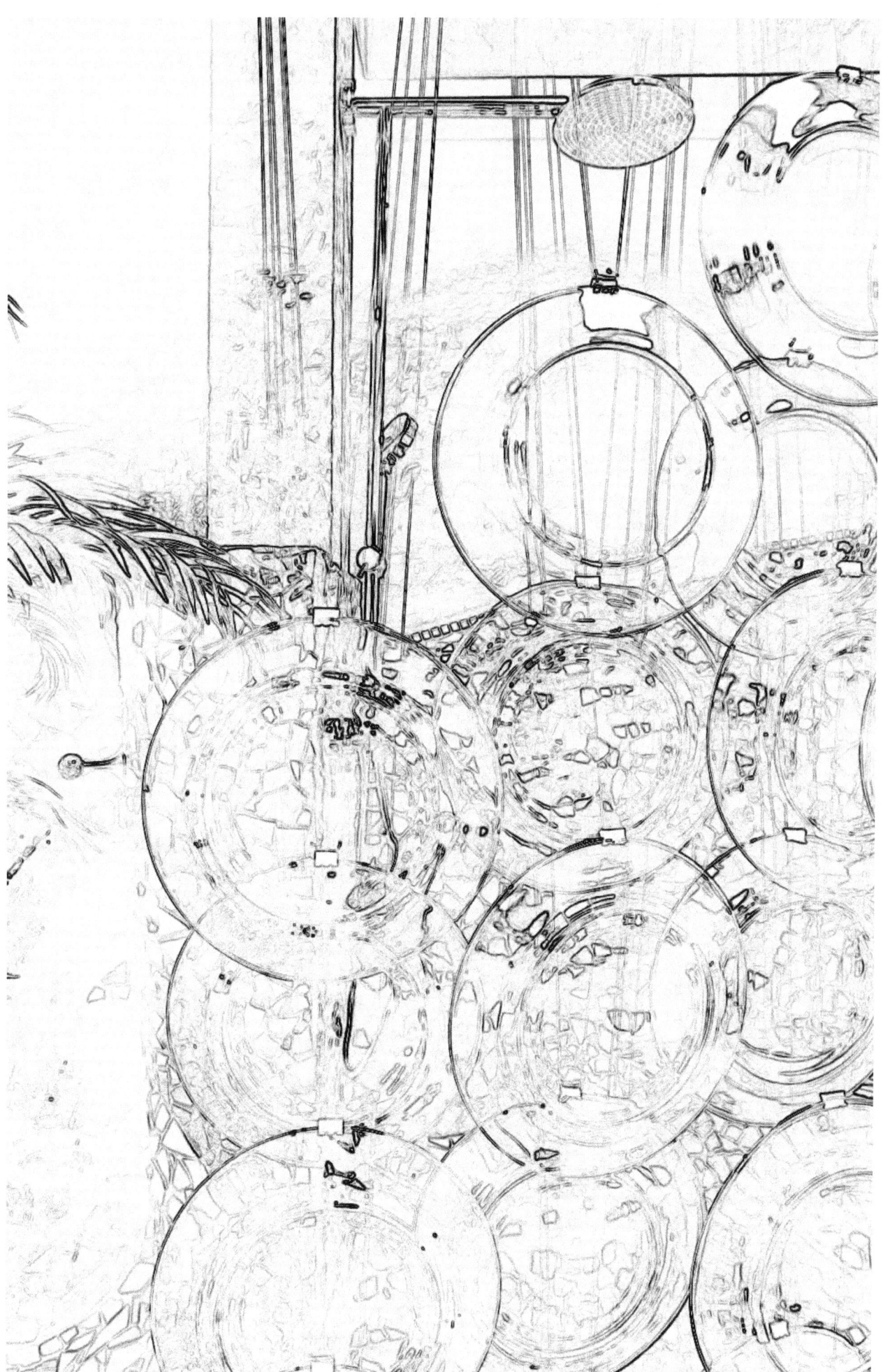

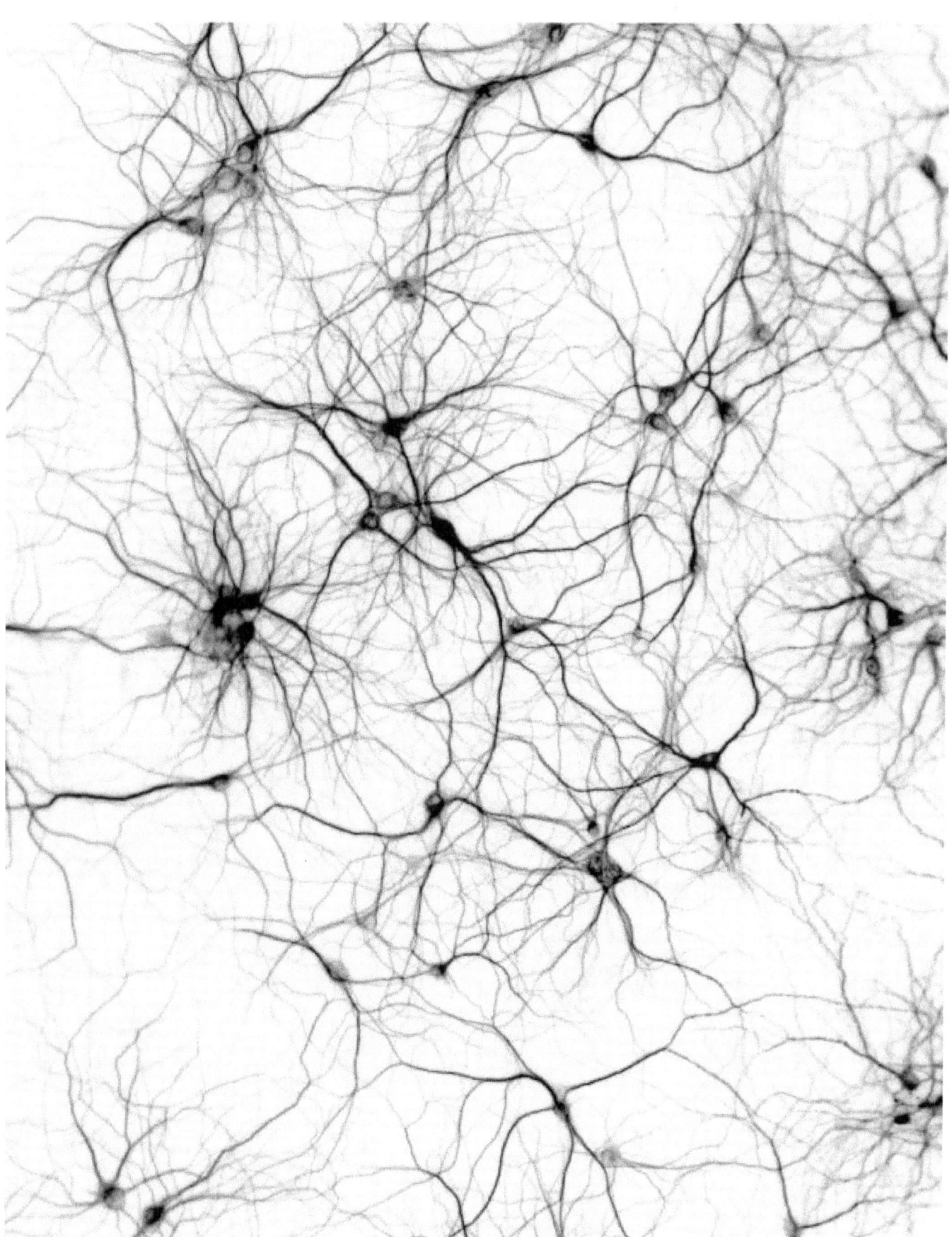

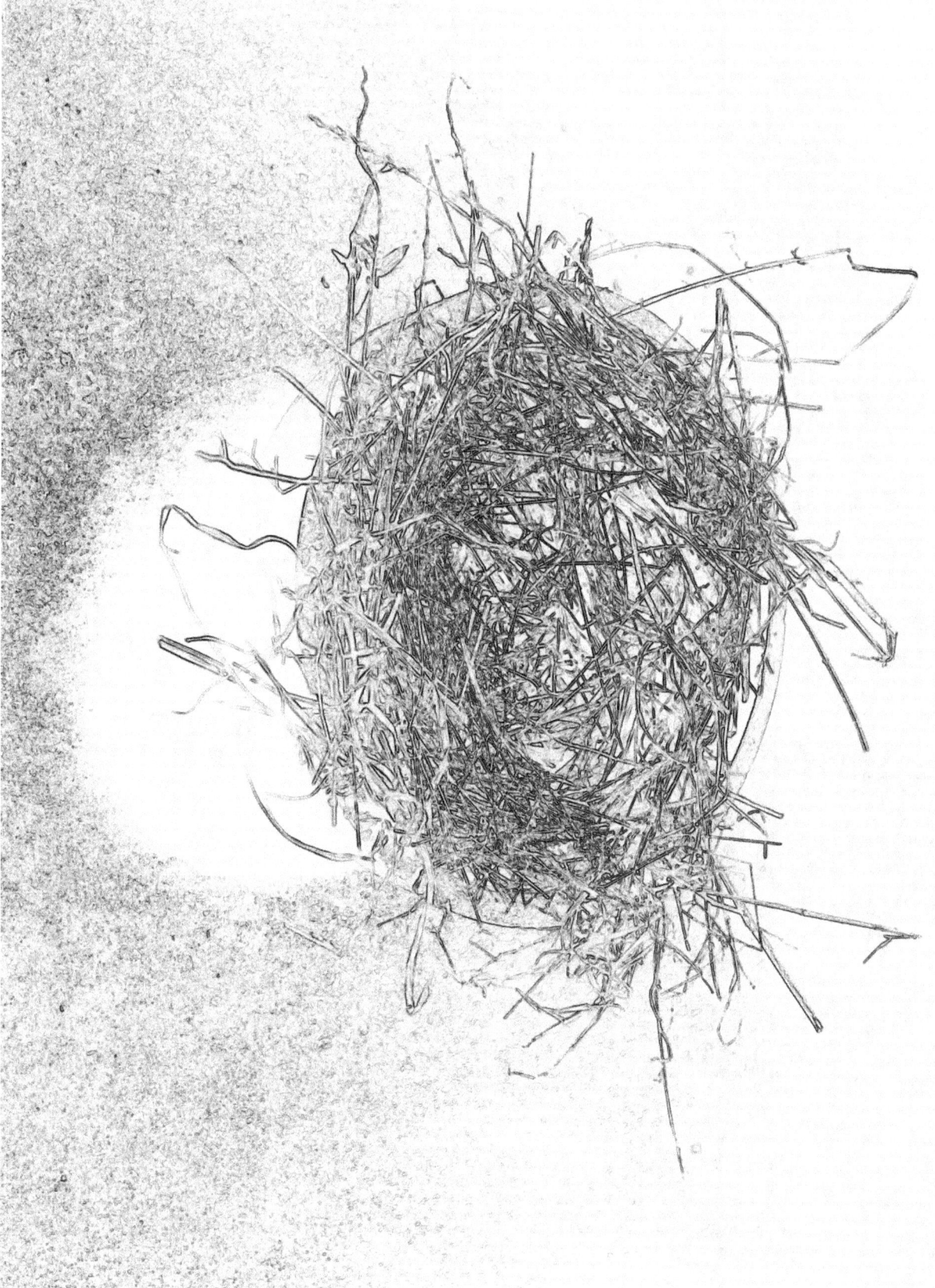

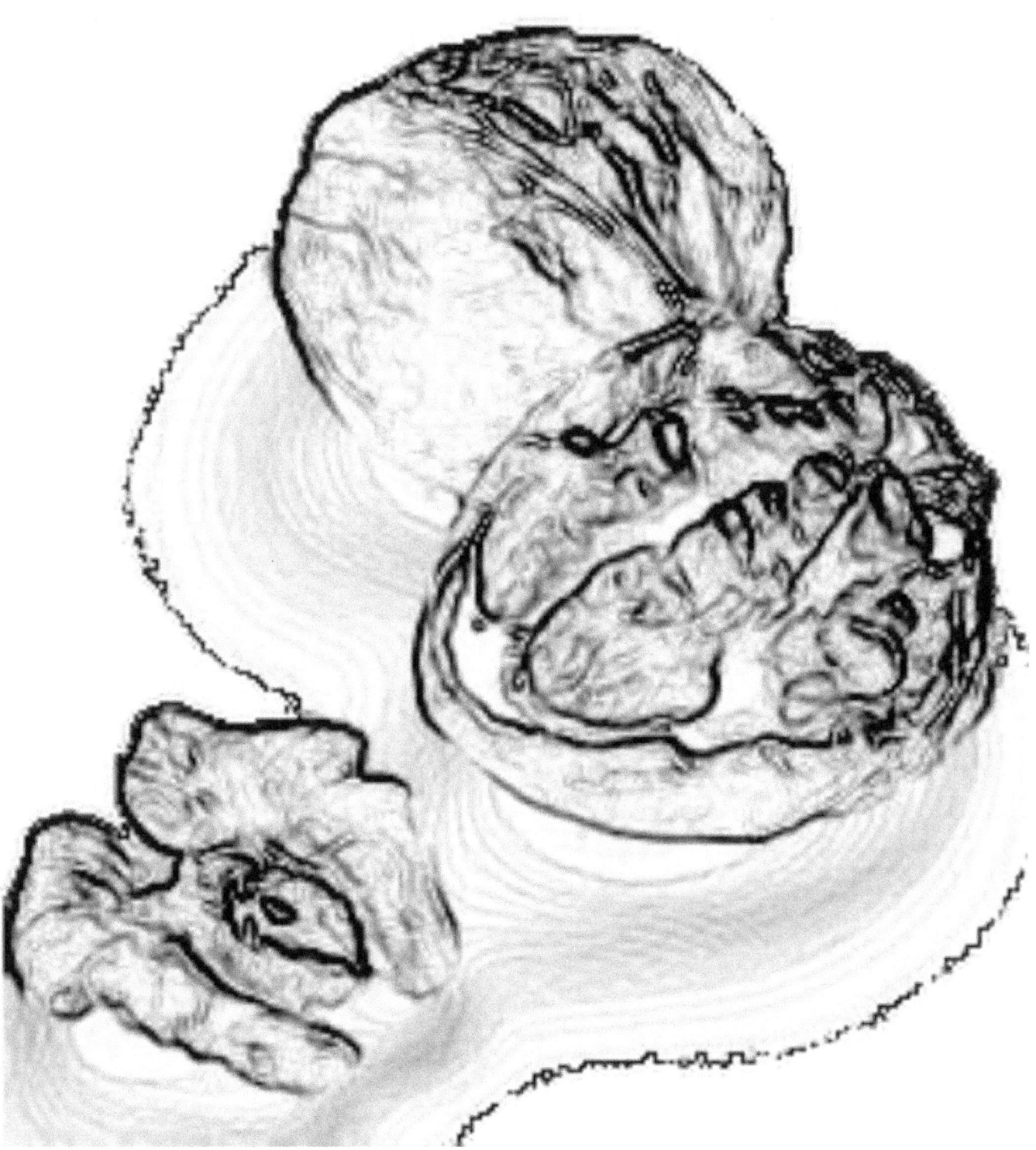

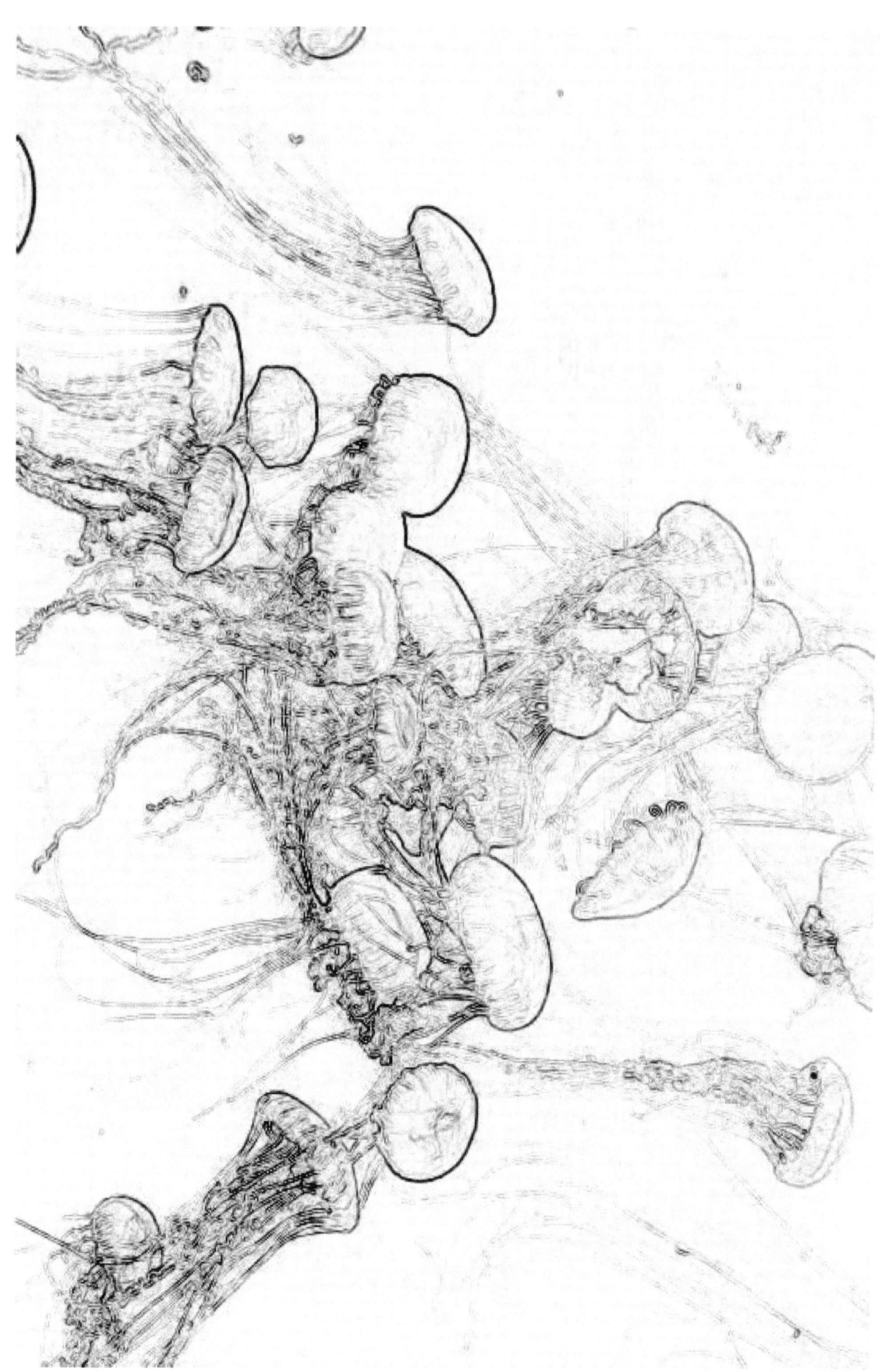

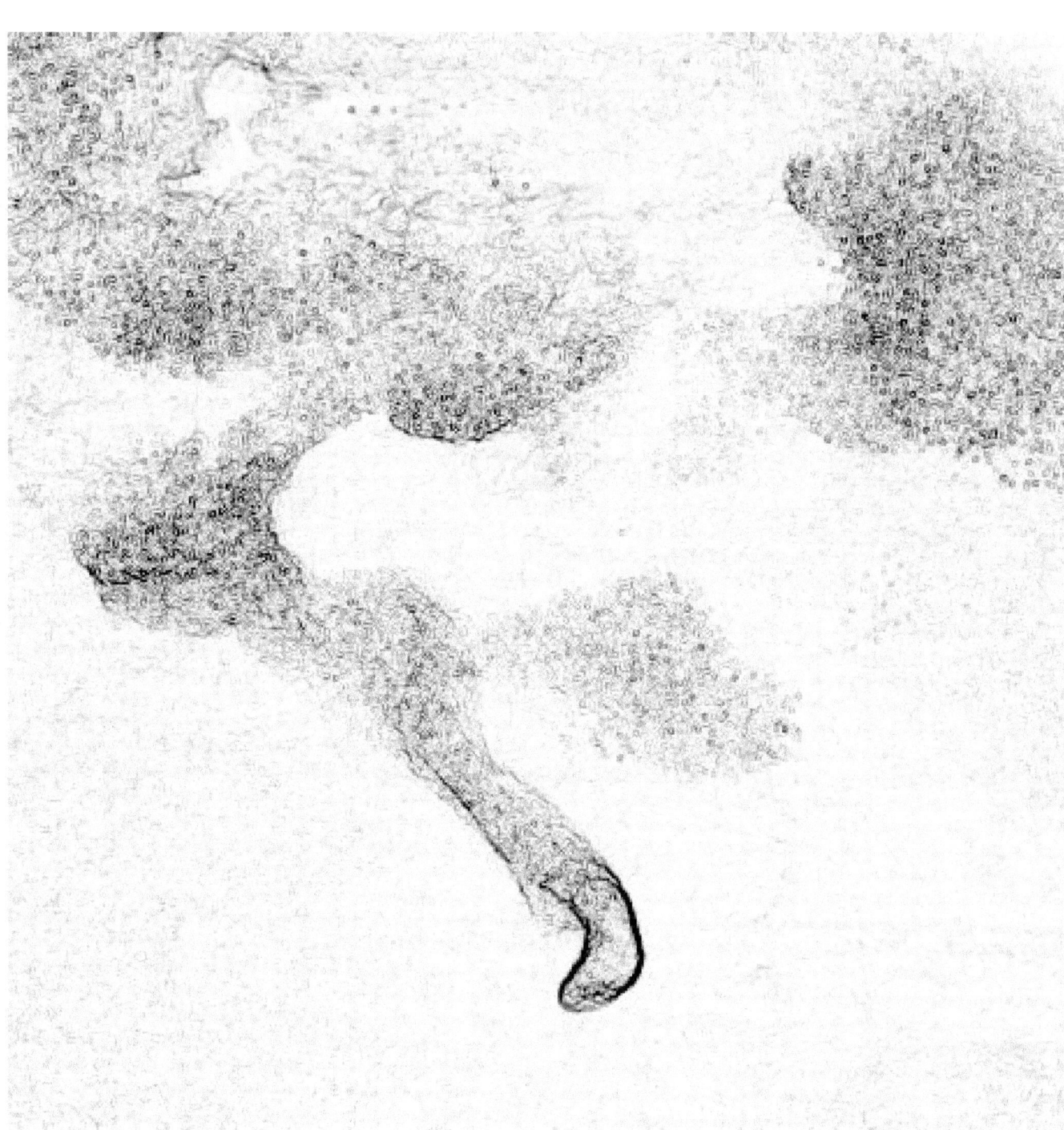

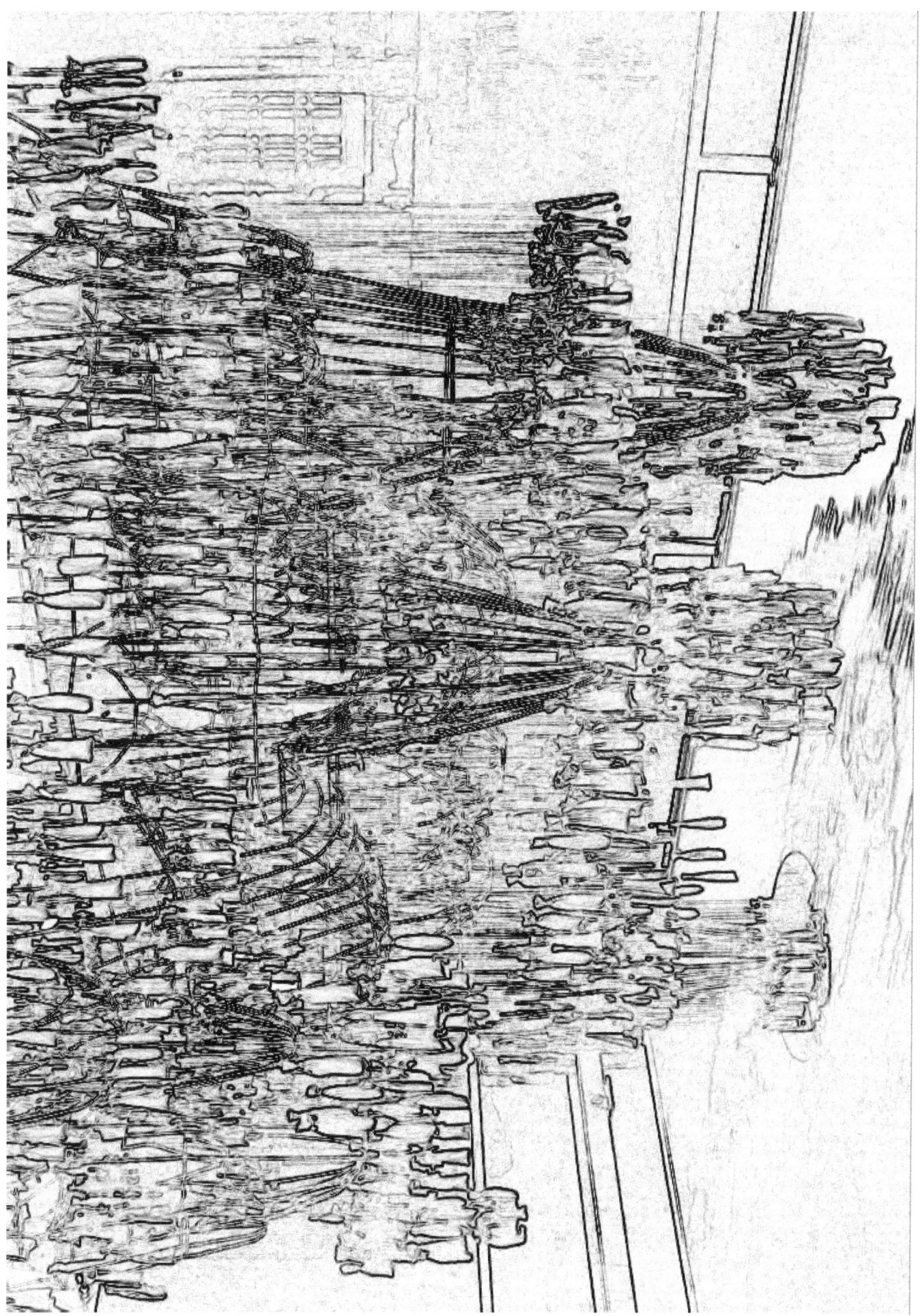

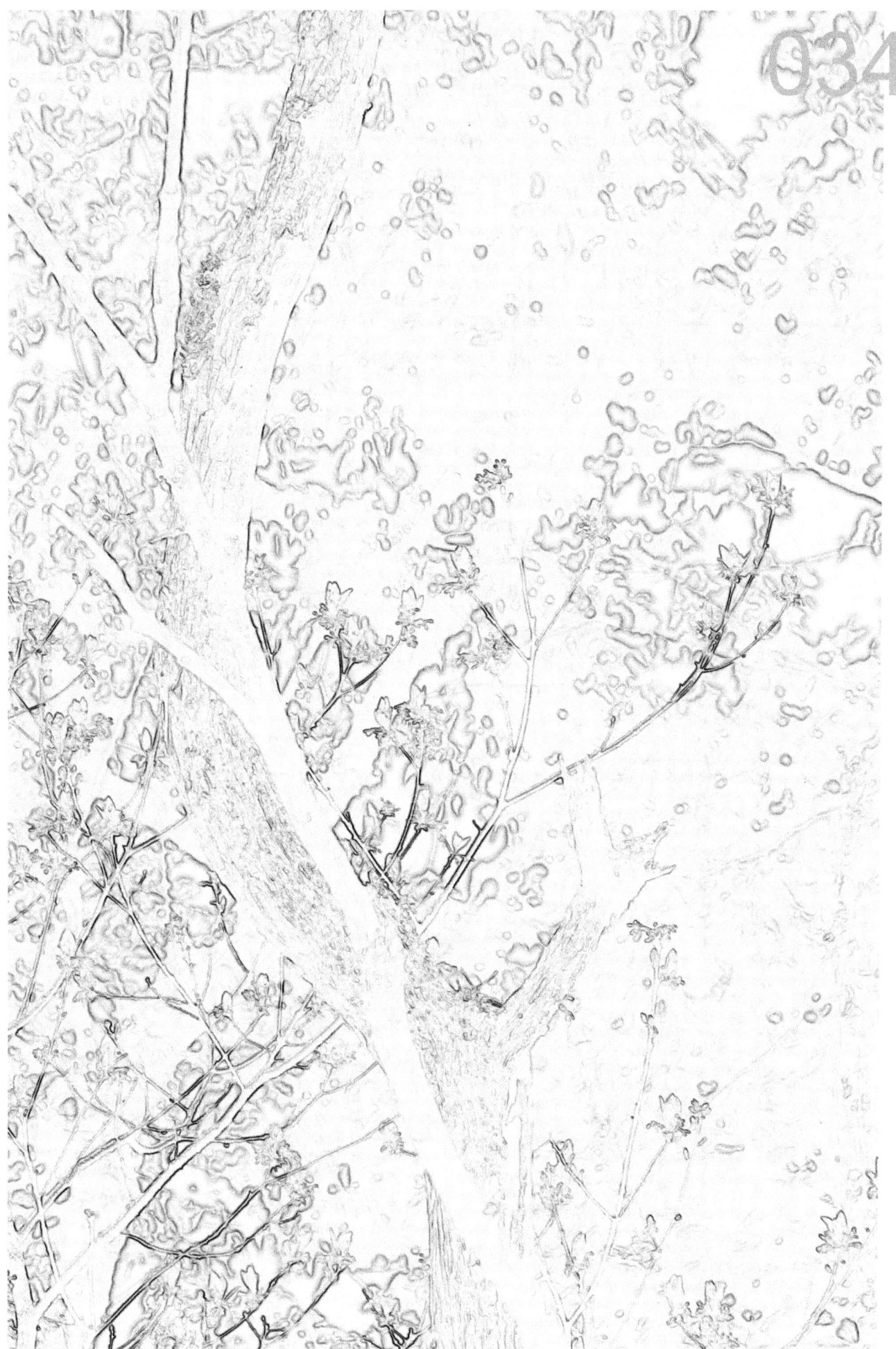

034

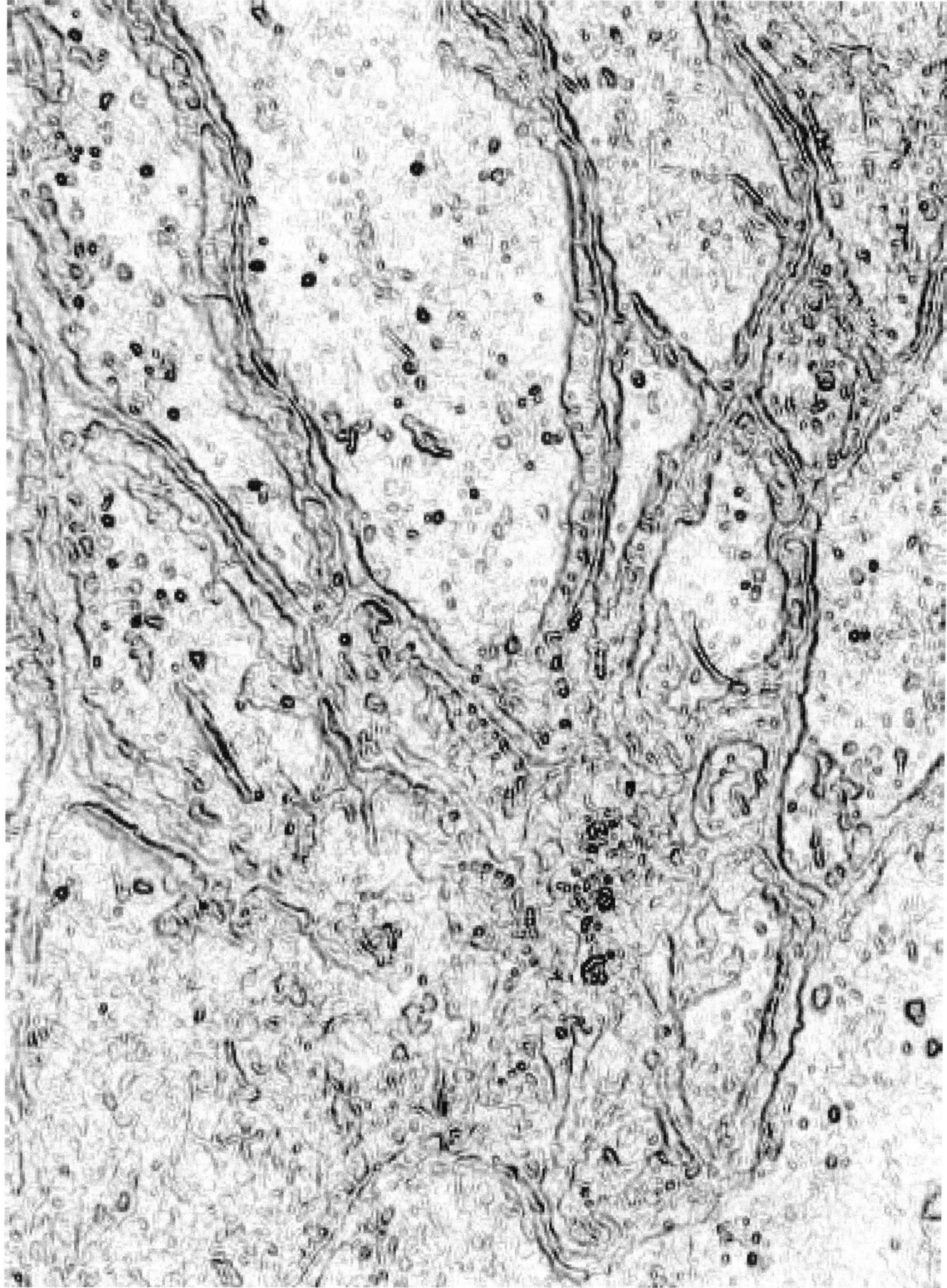

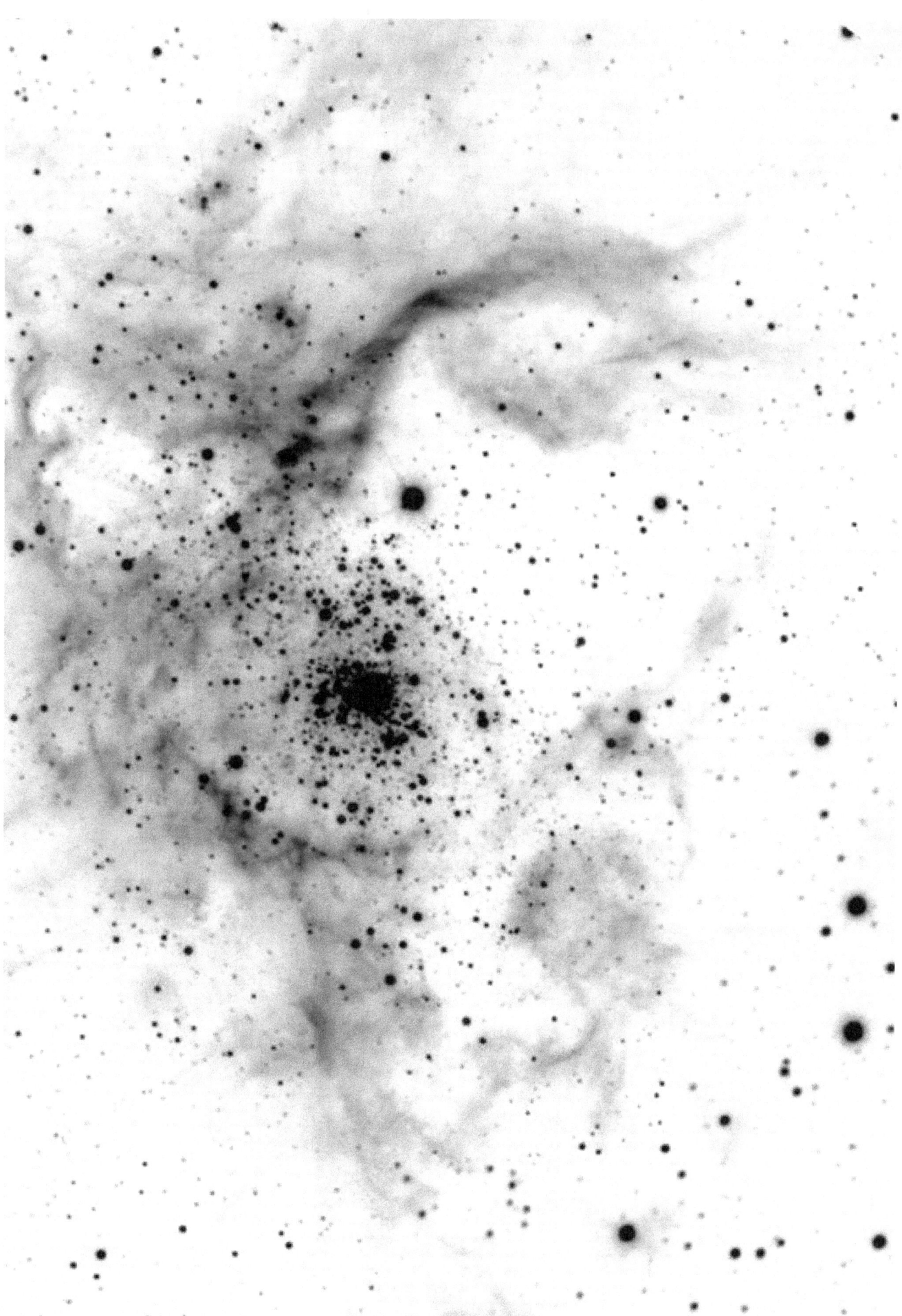

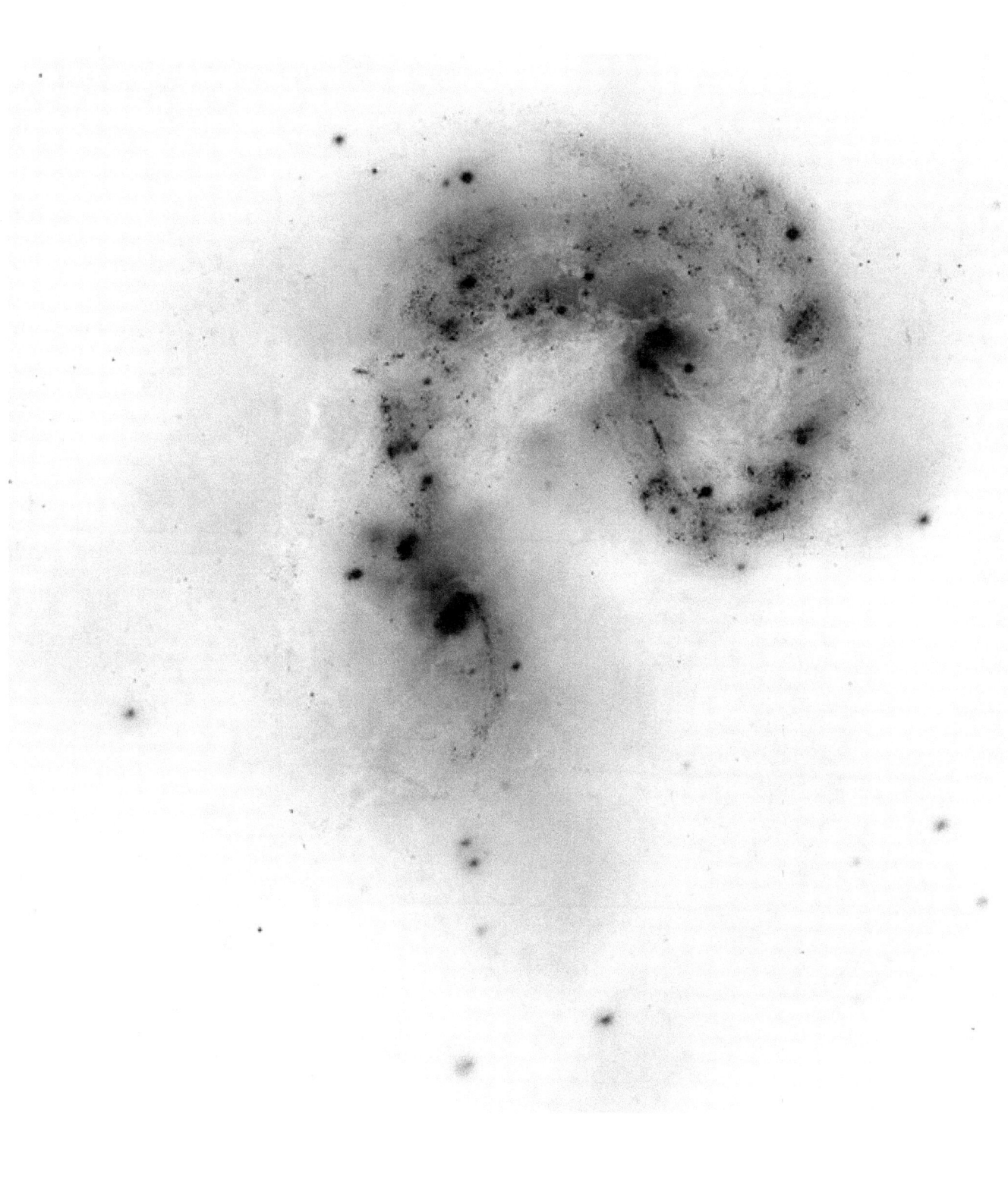

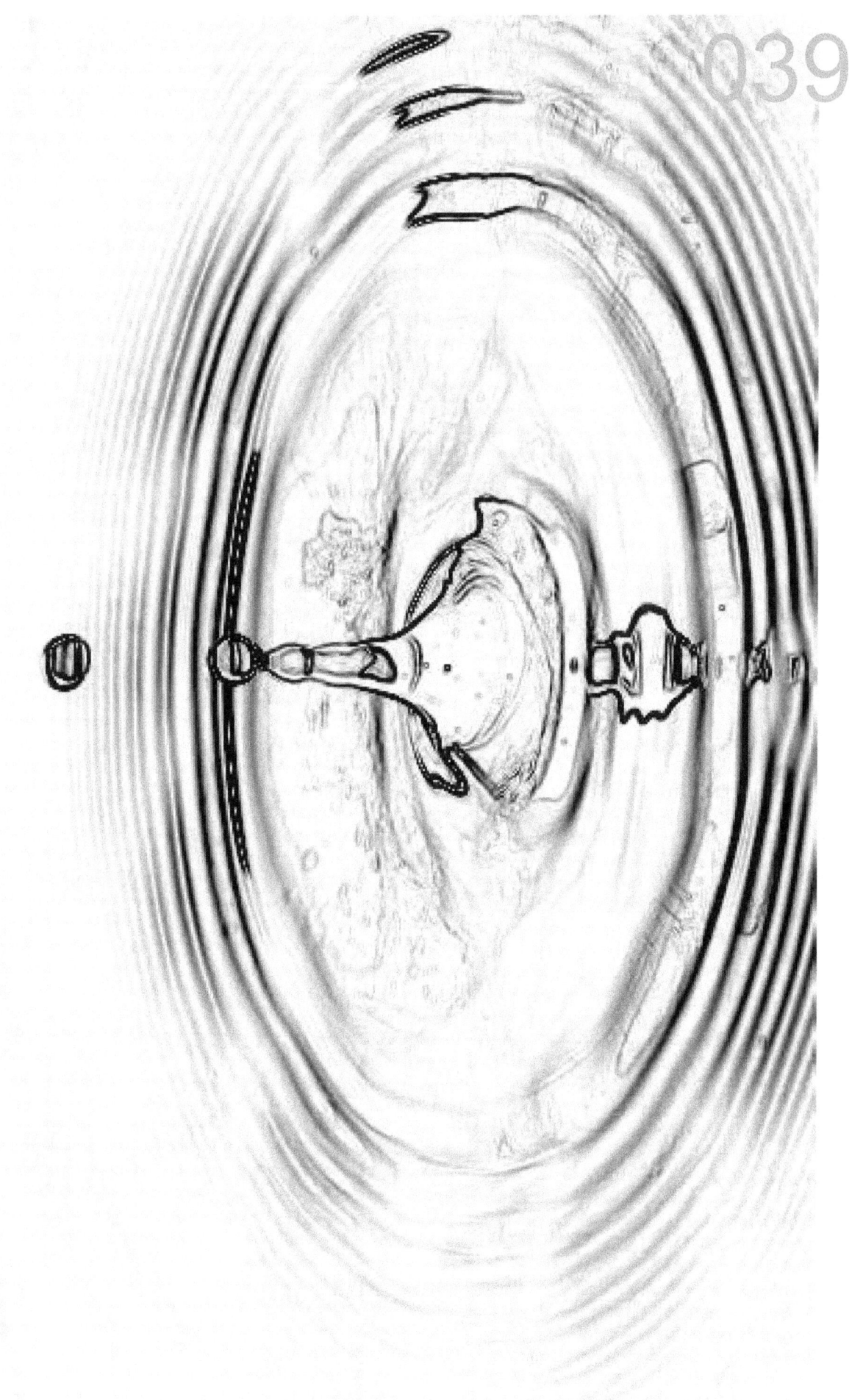

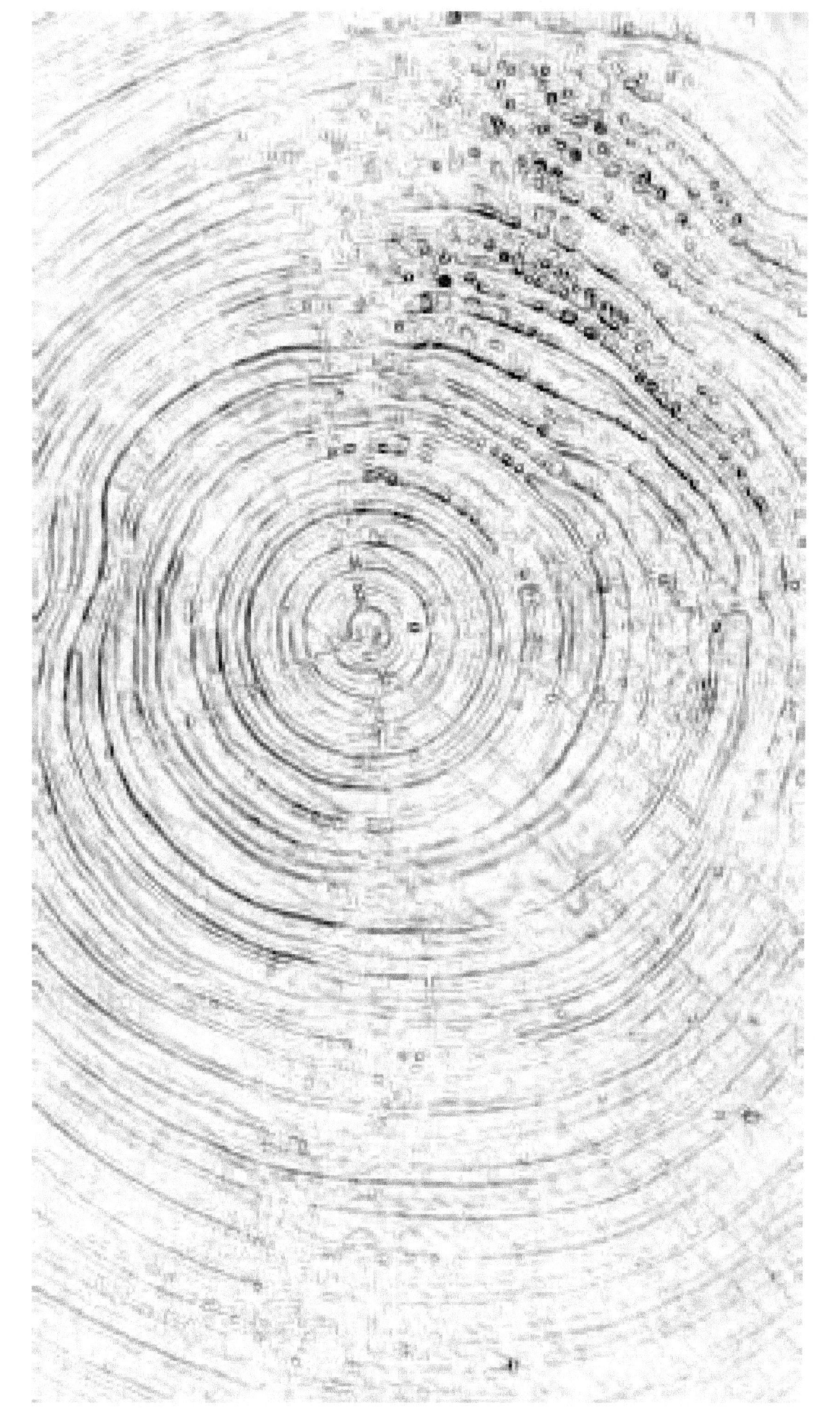

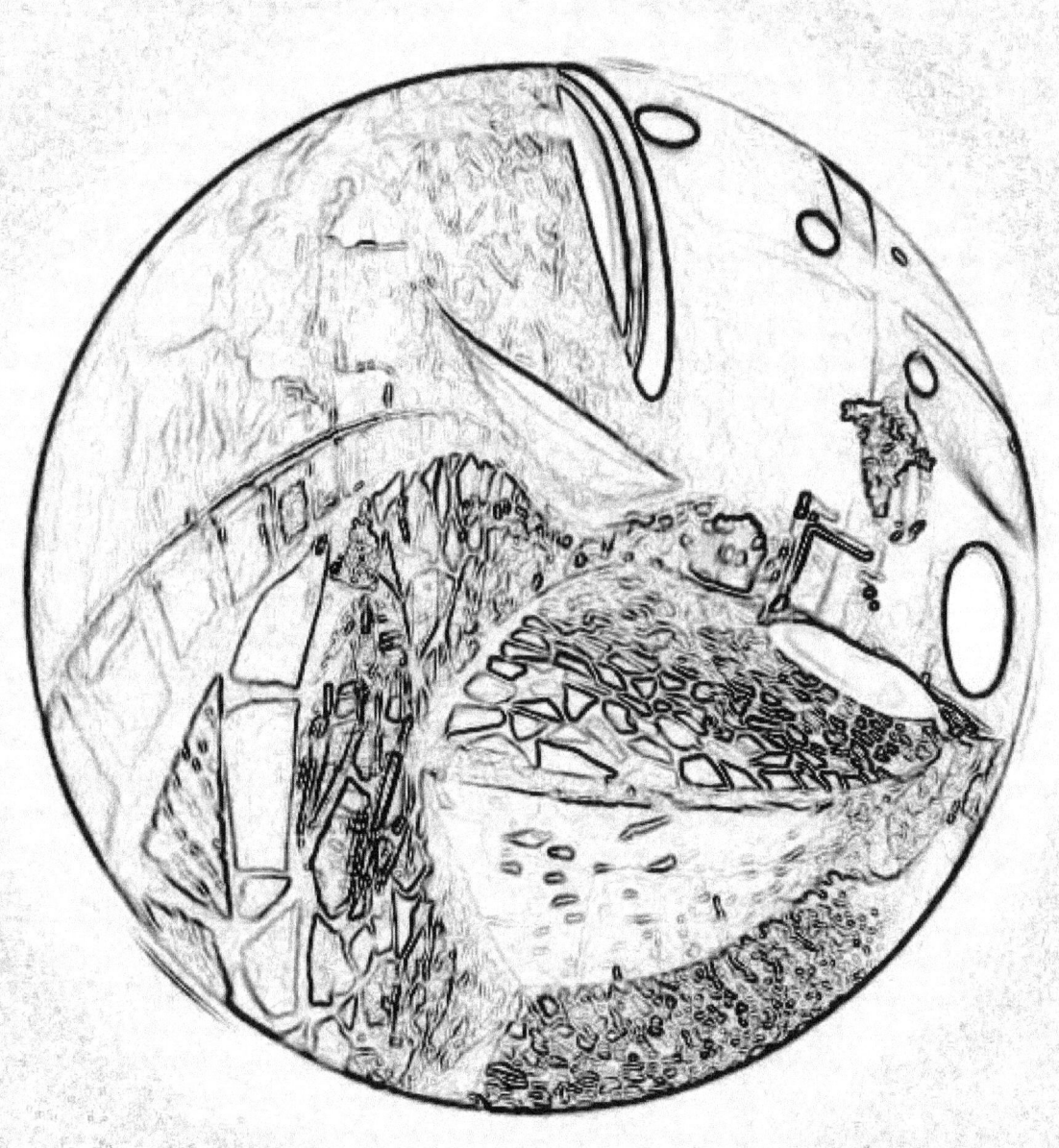

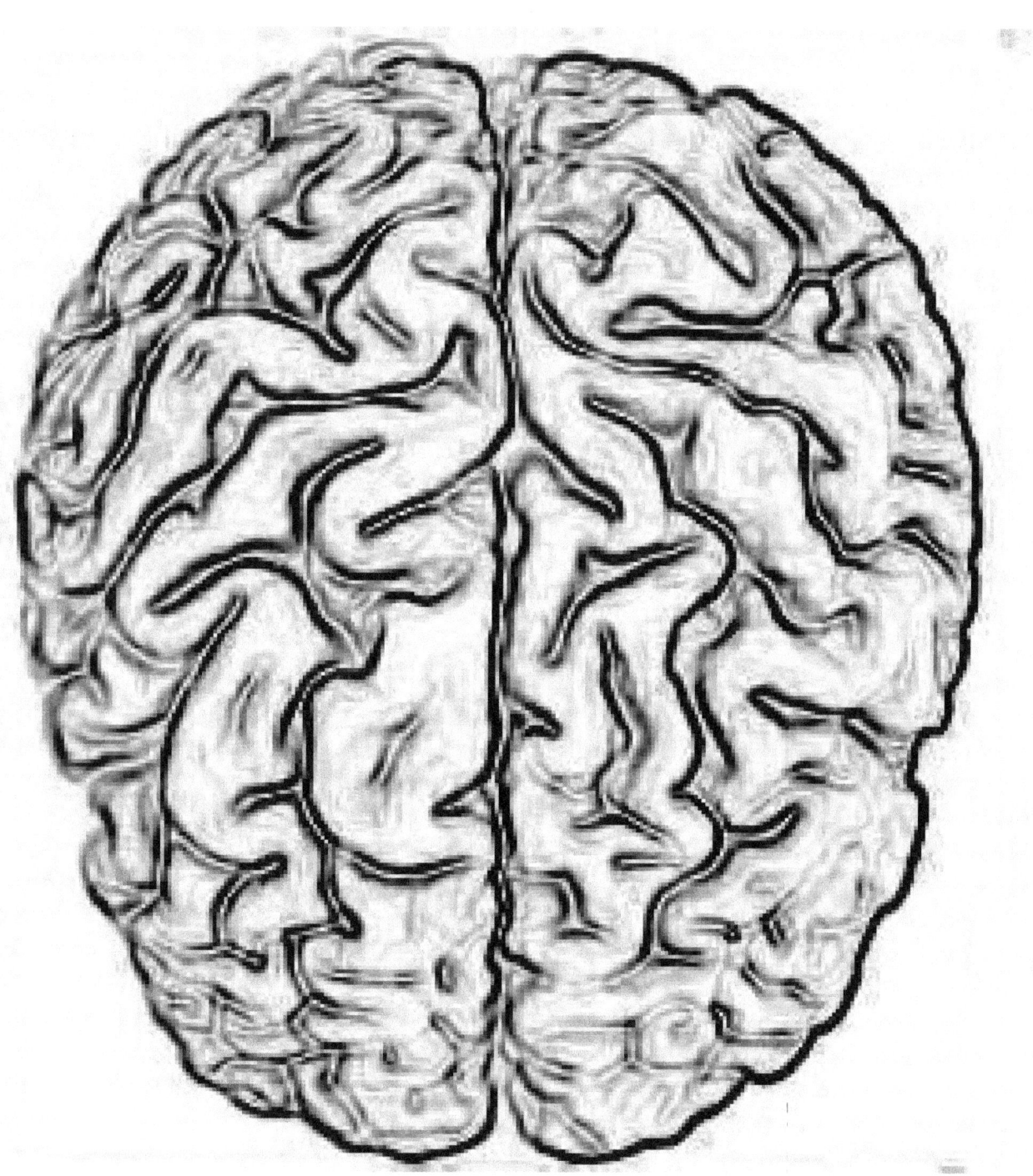

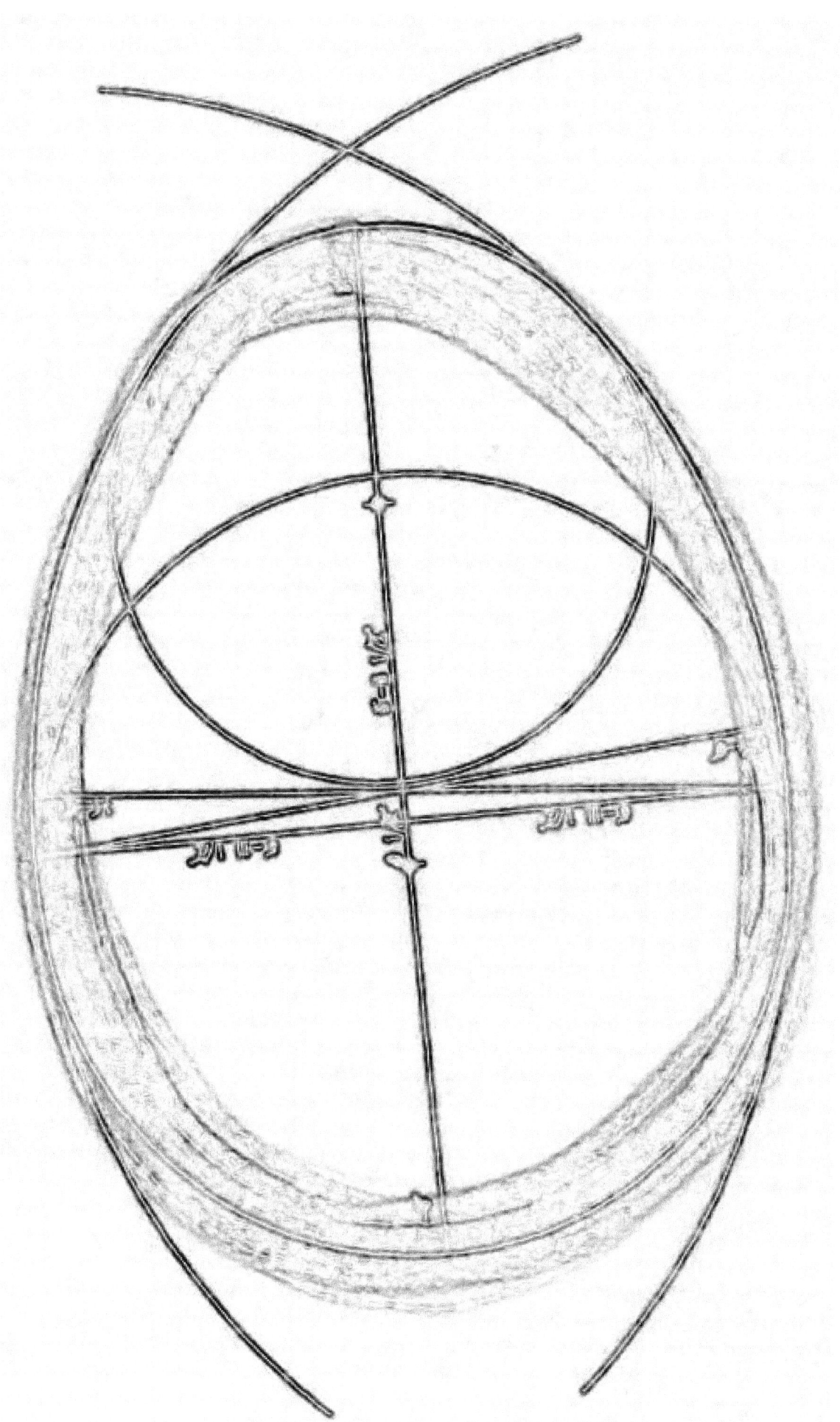

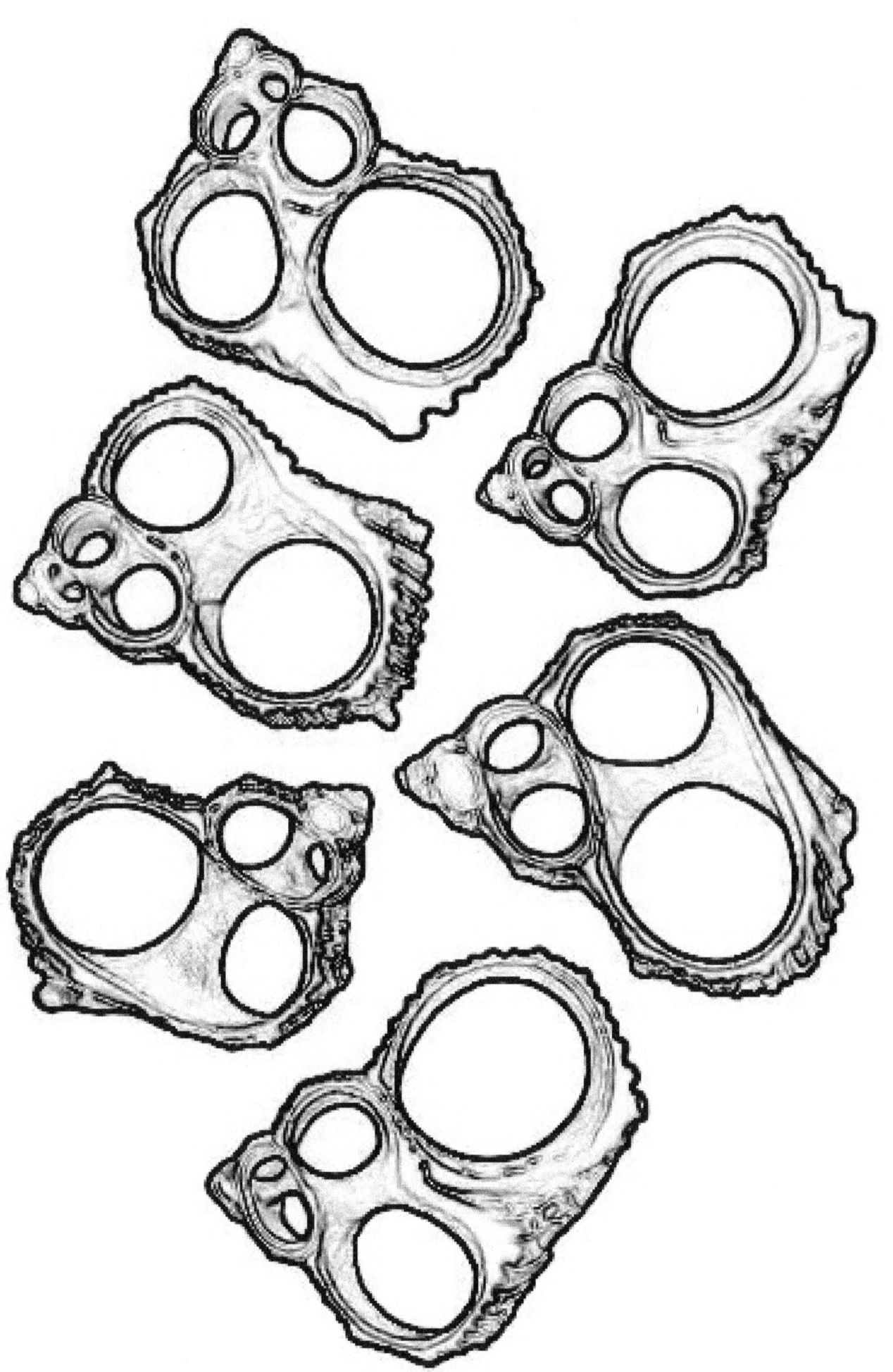

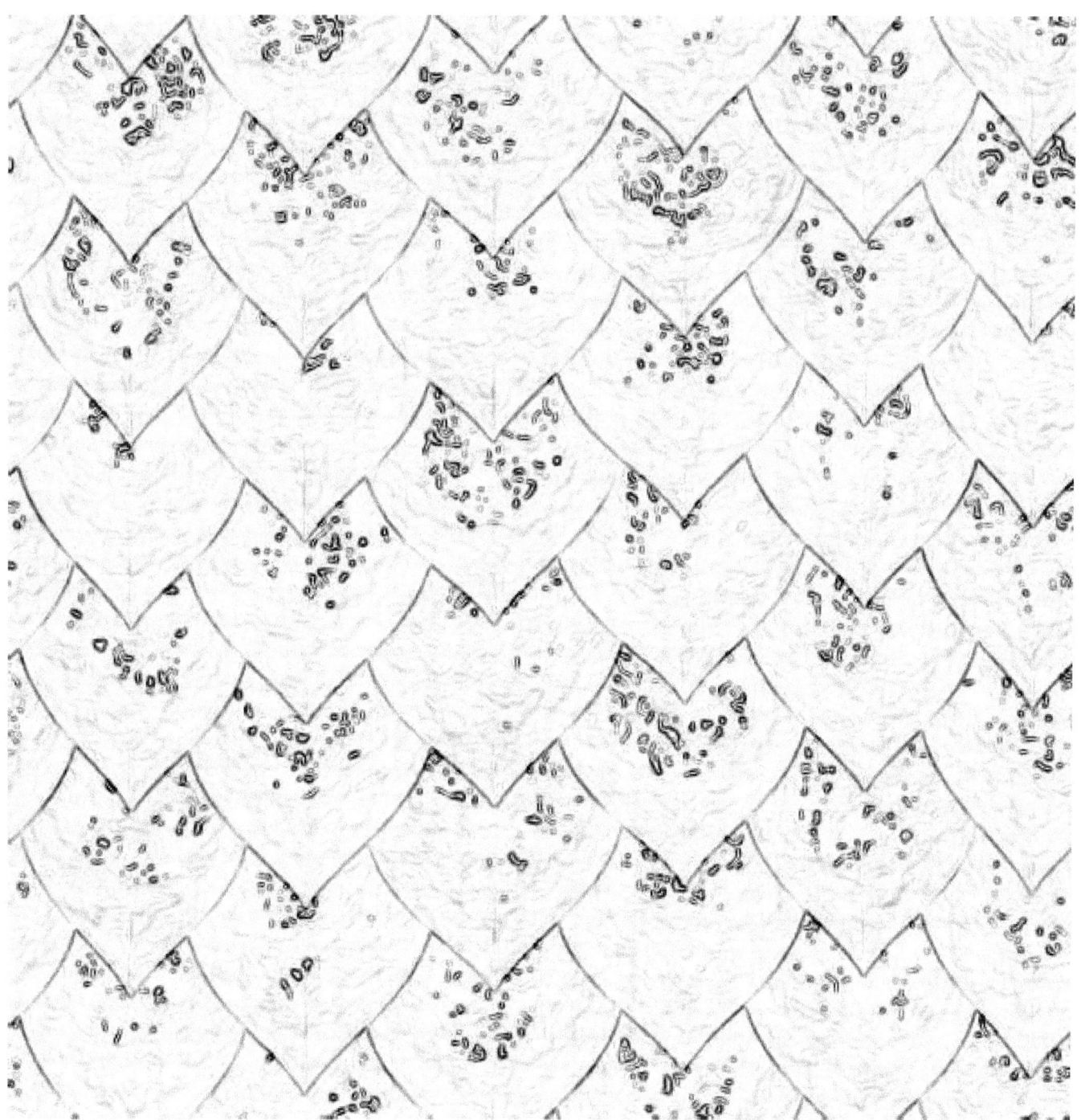

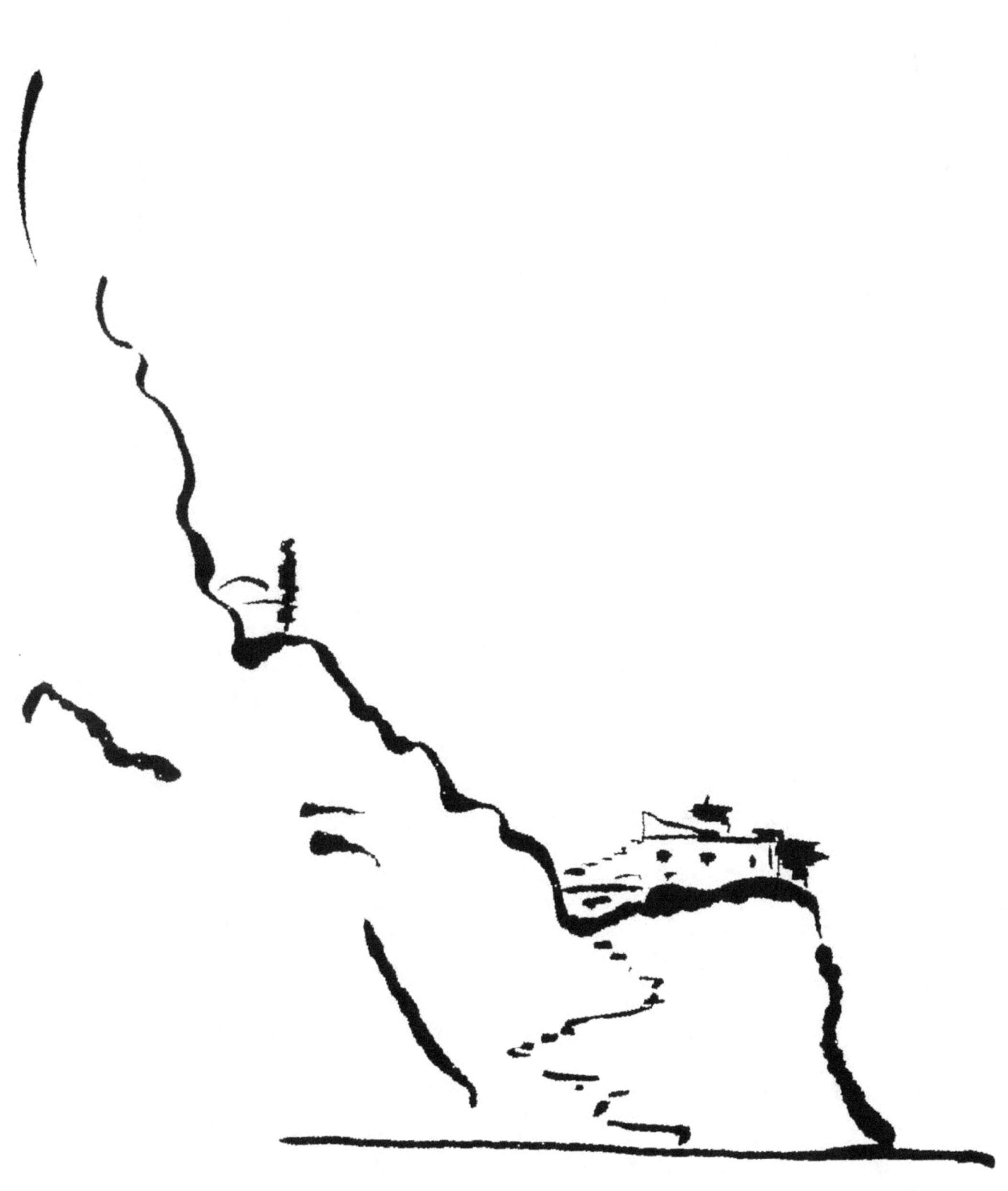

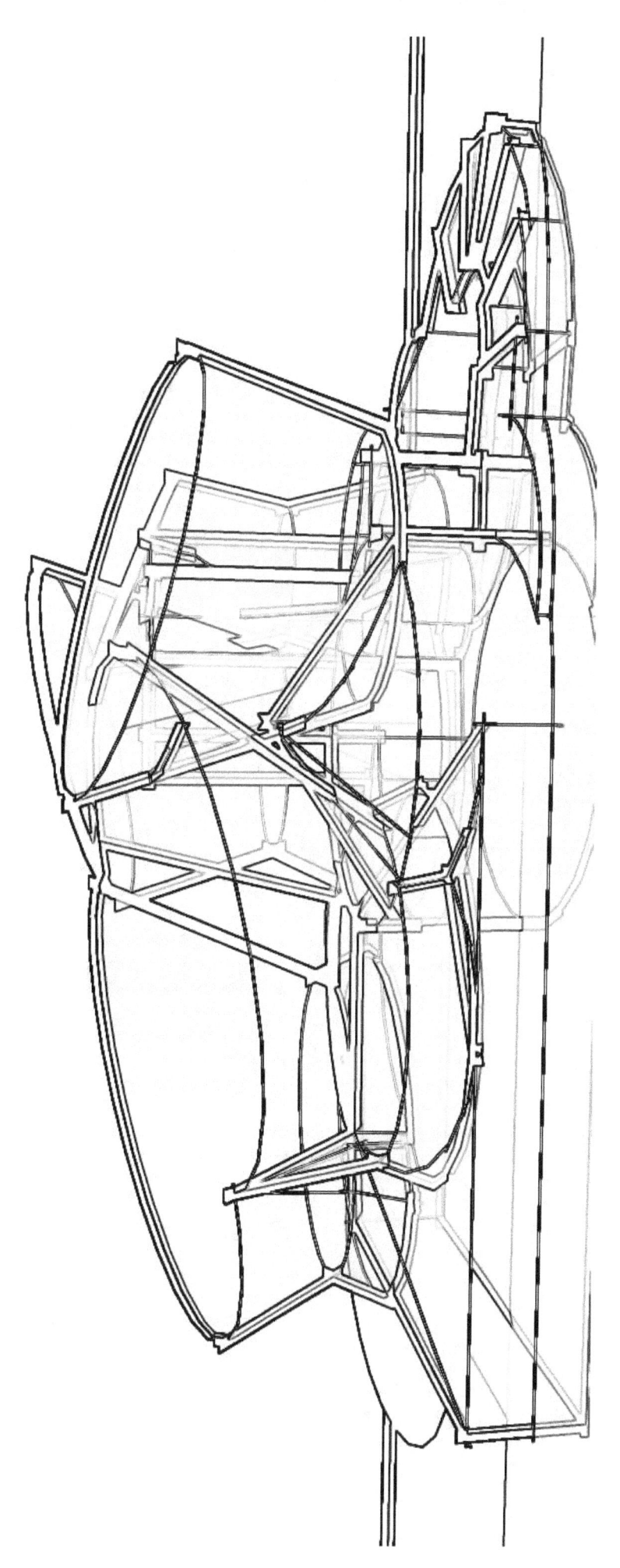

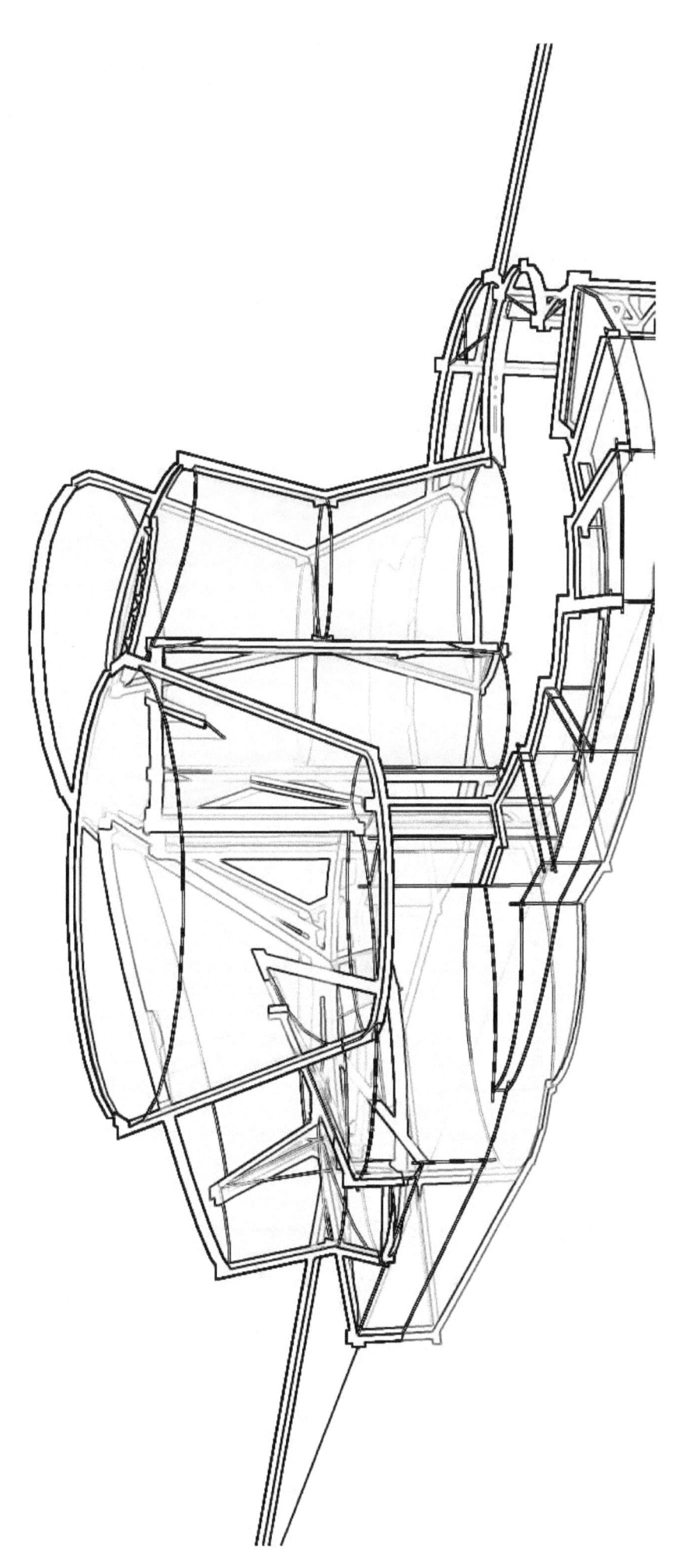

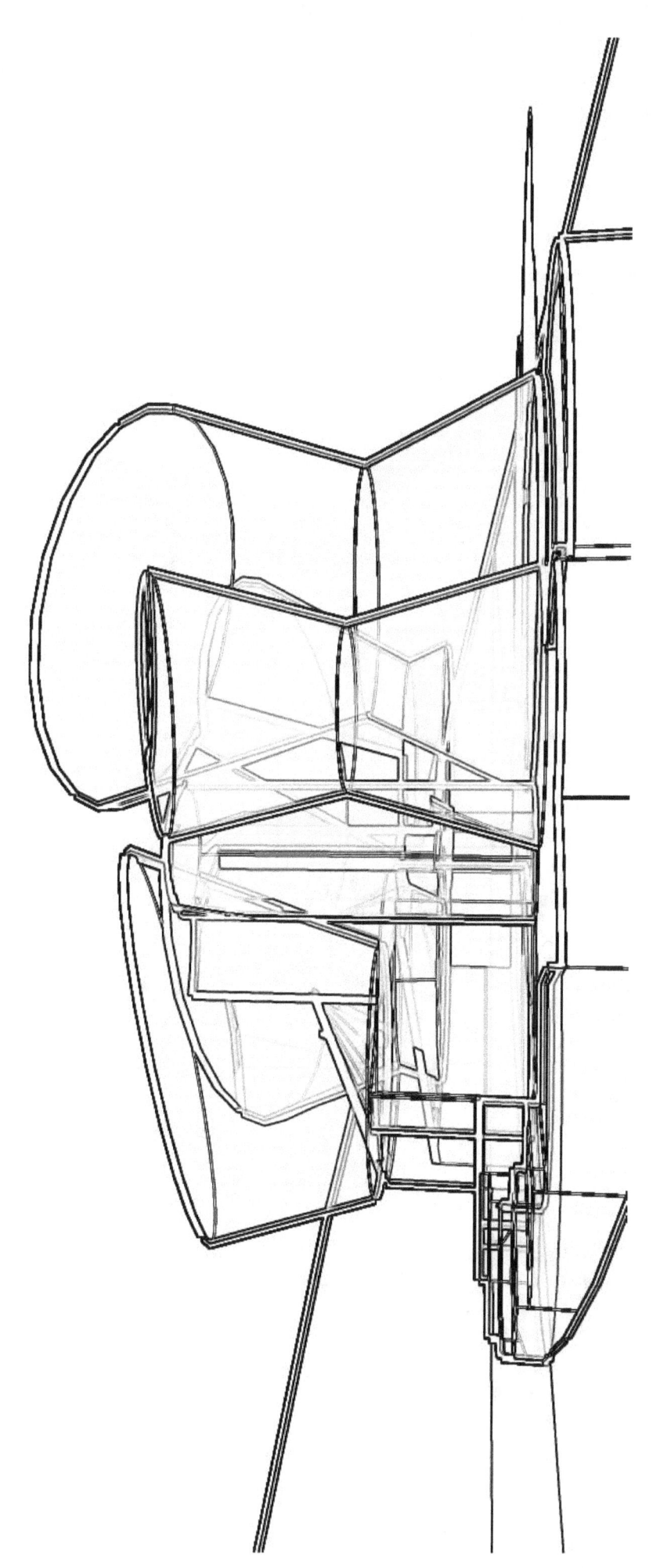

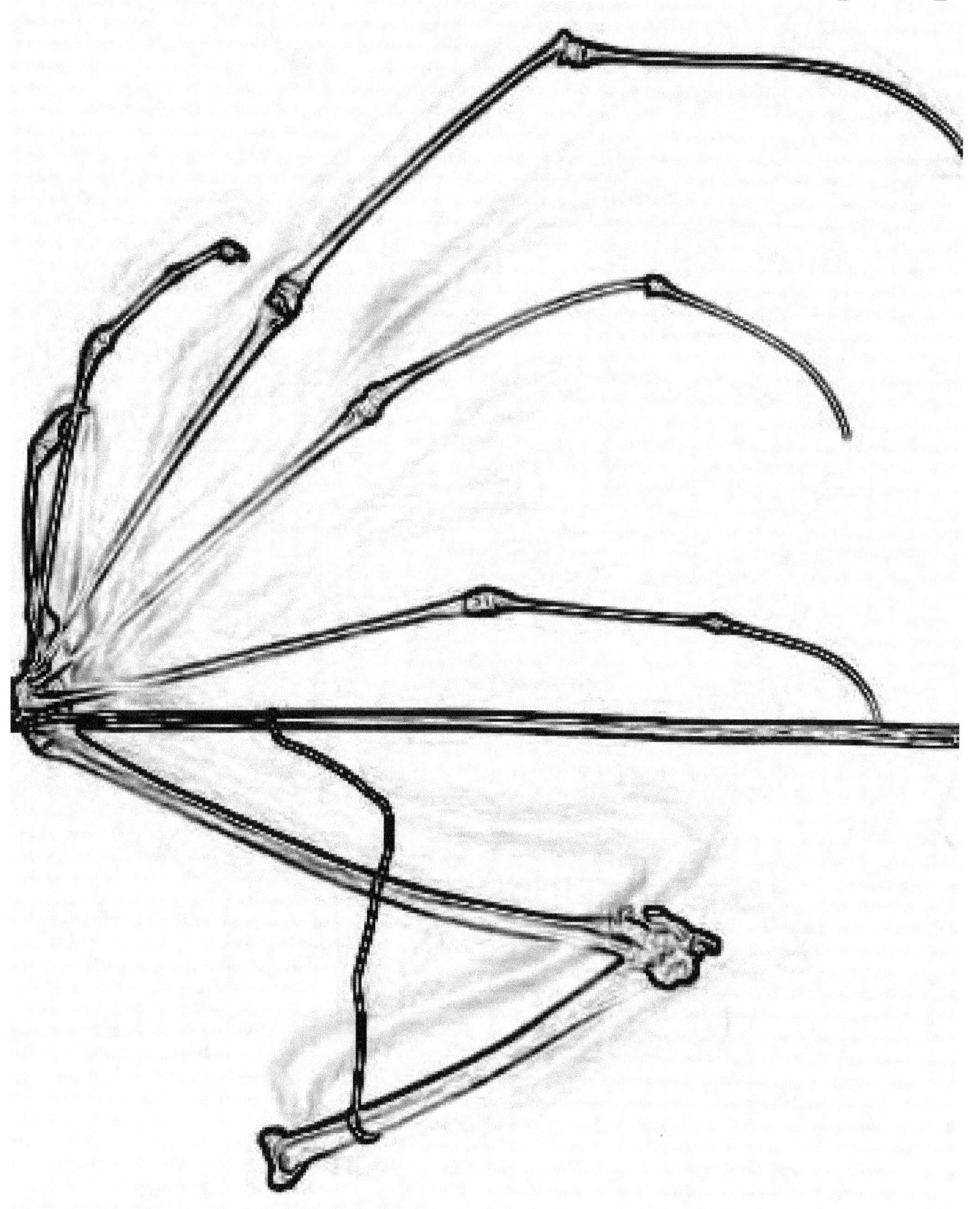

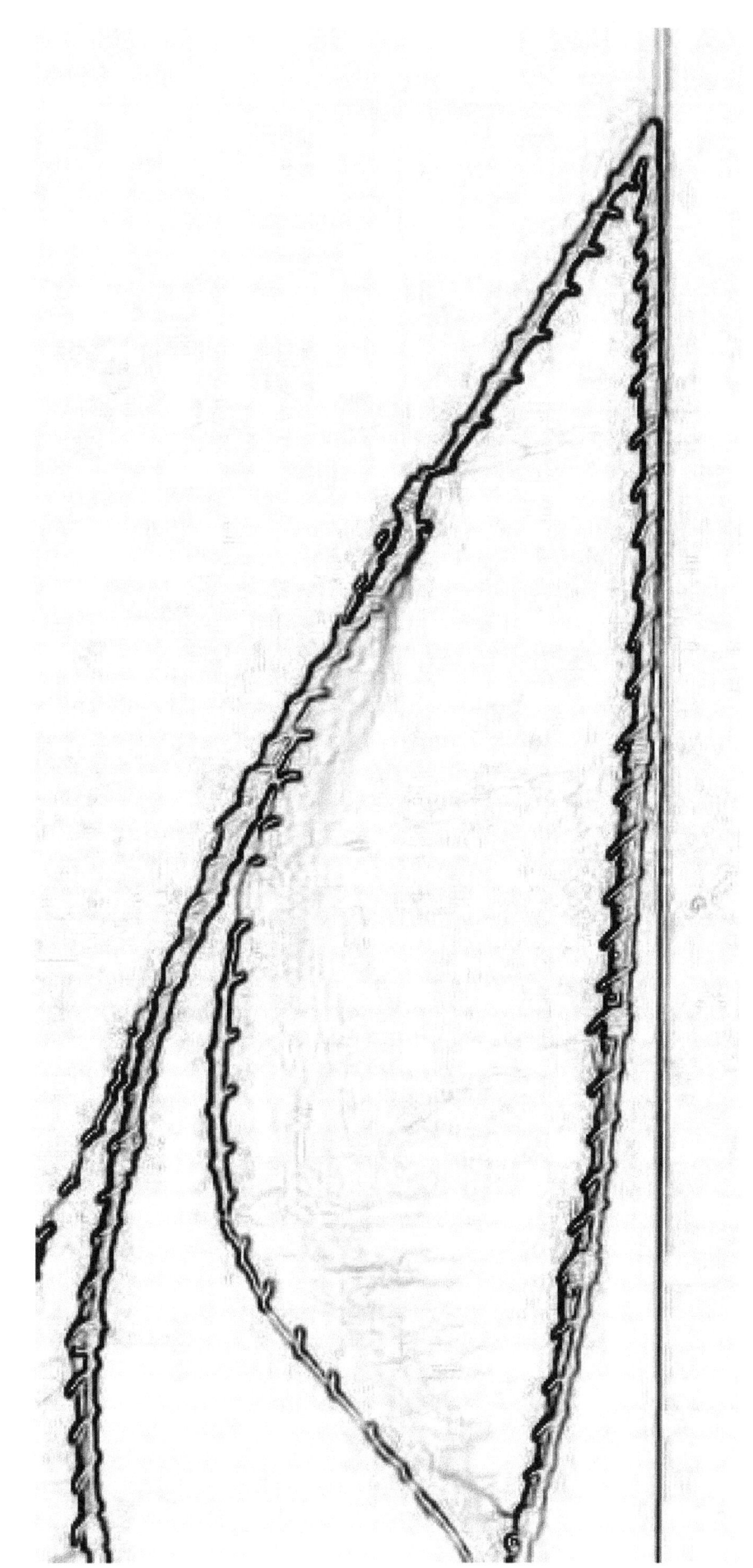

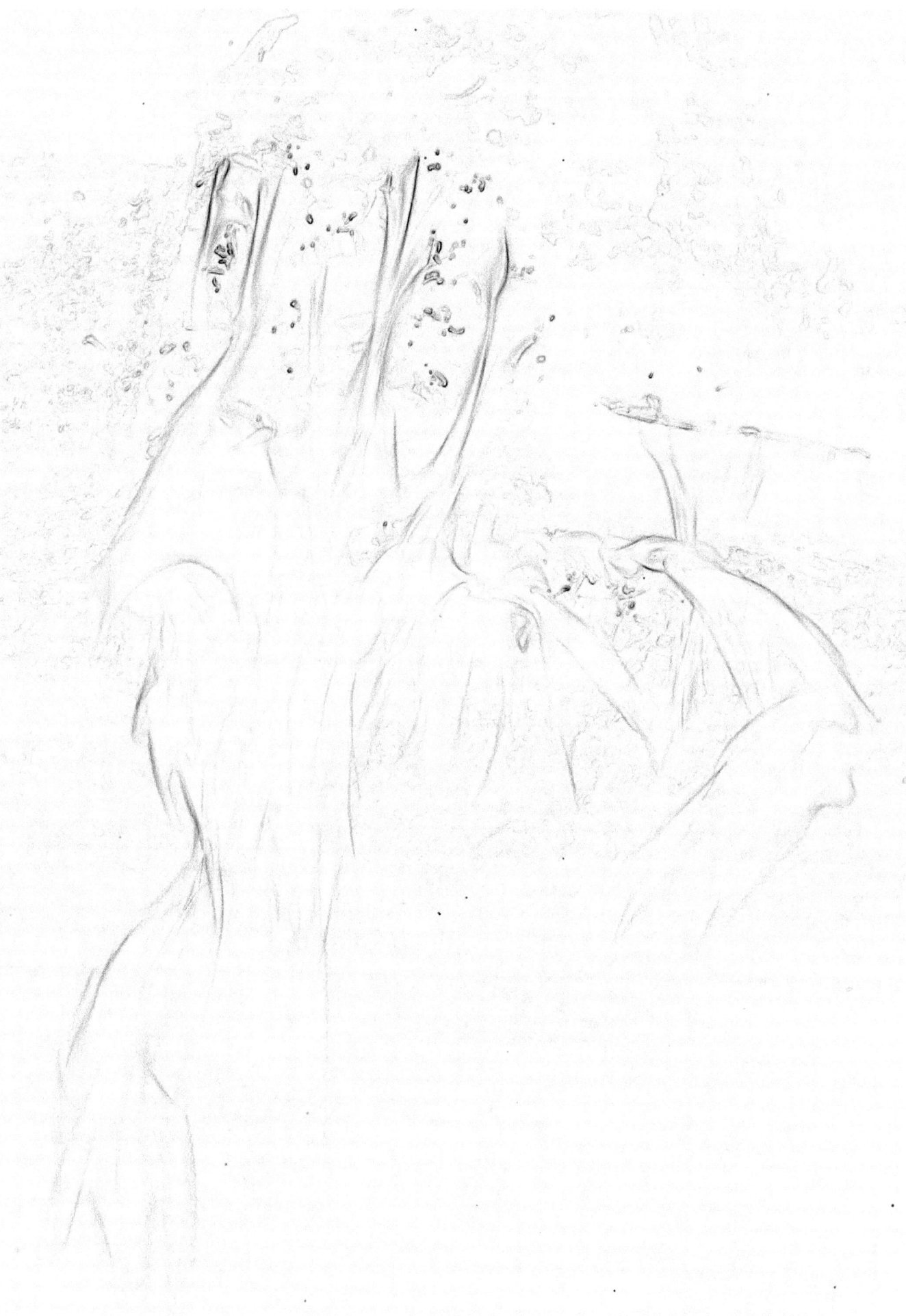

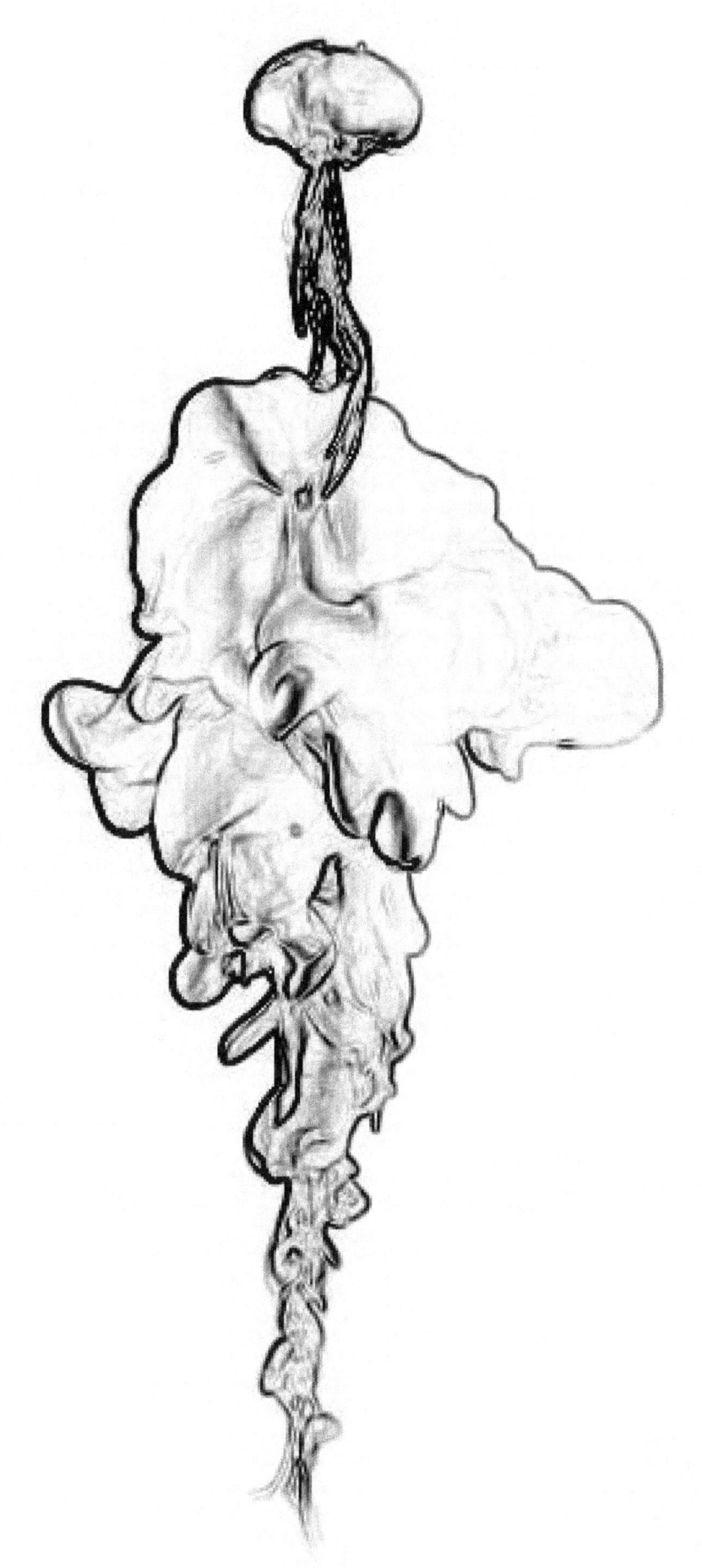

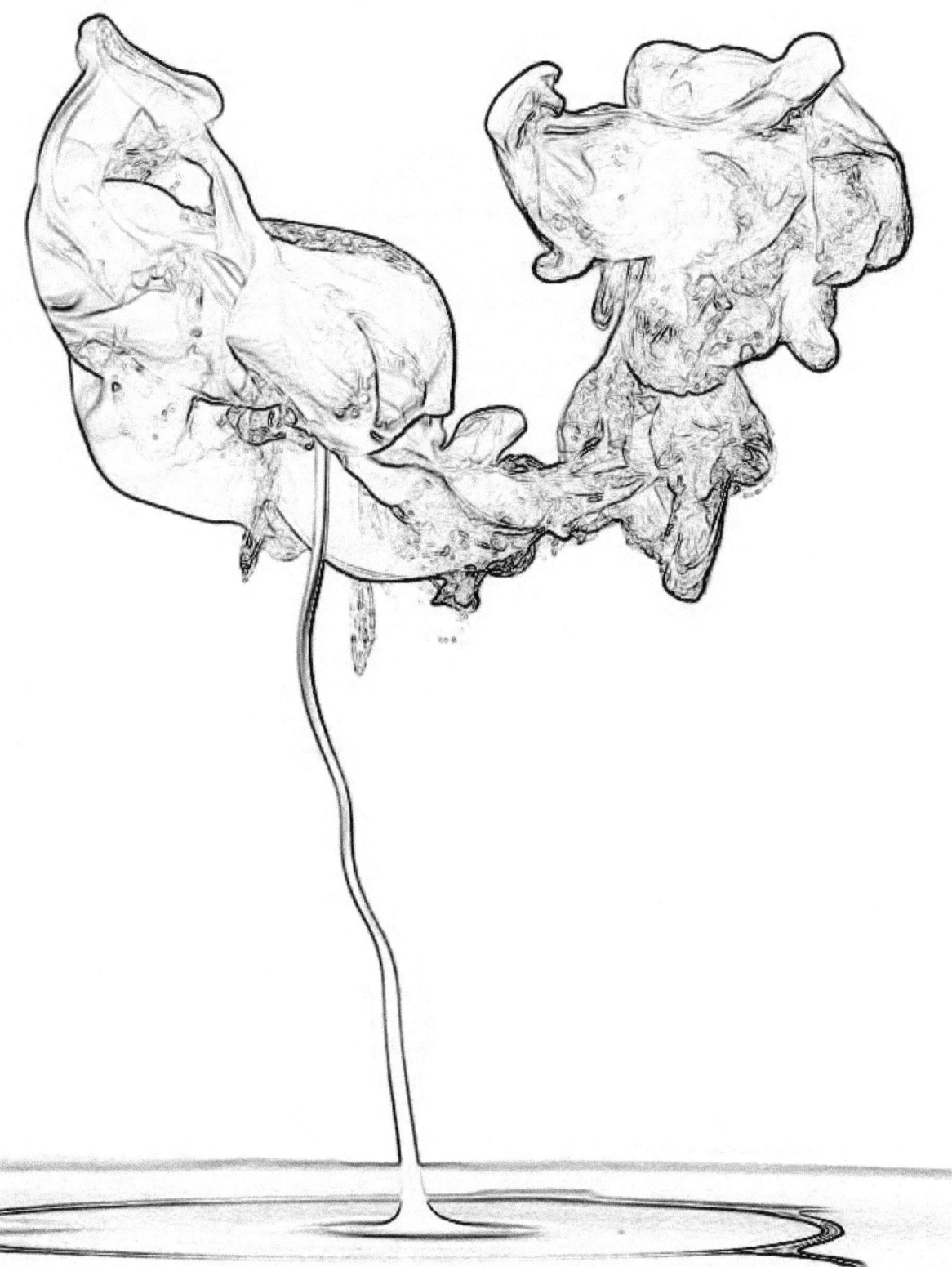

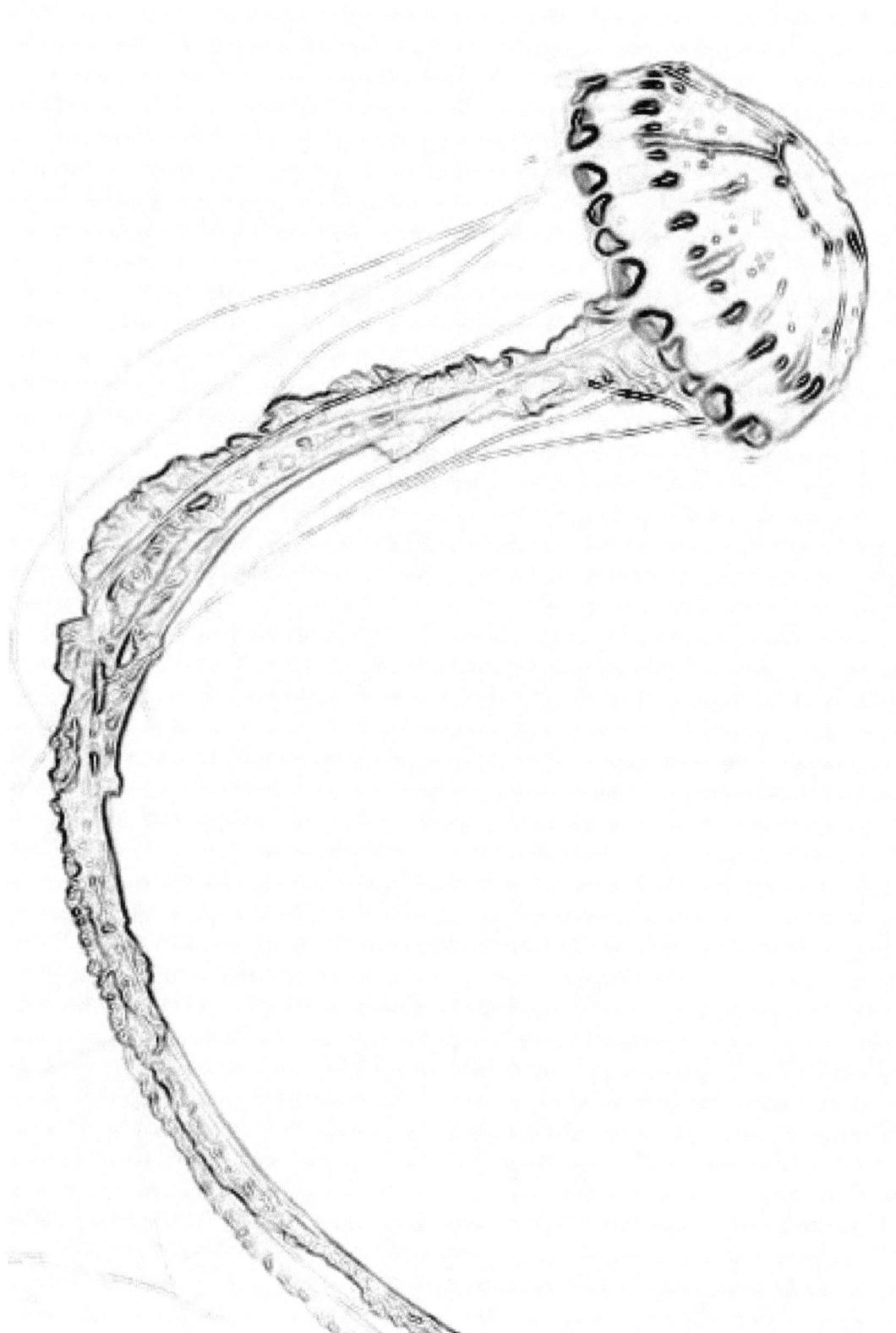

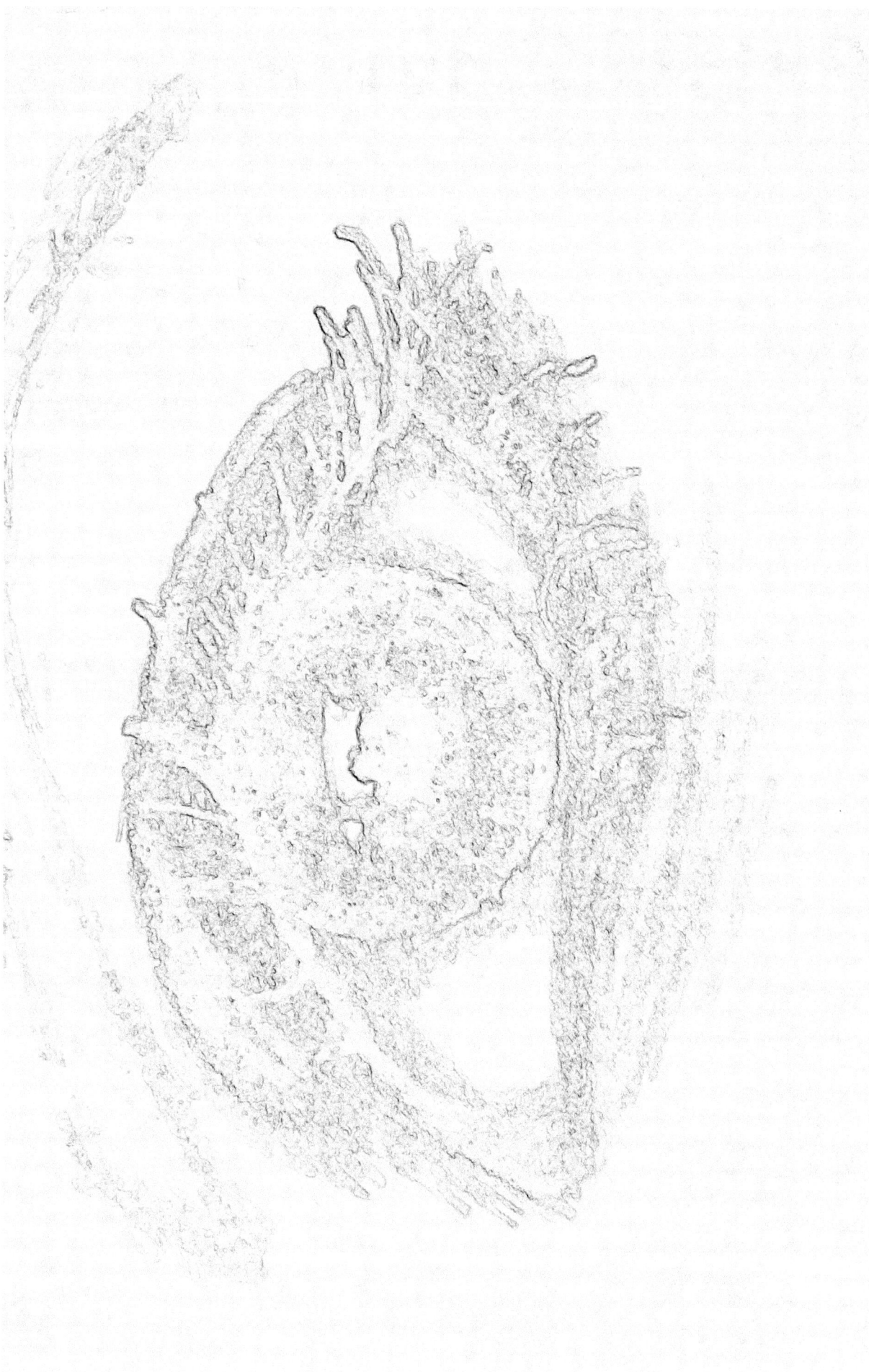

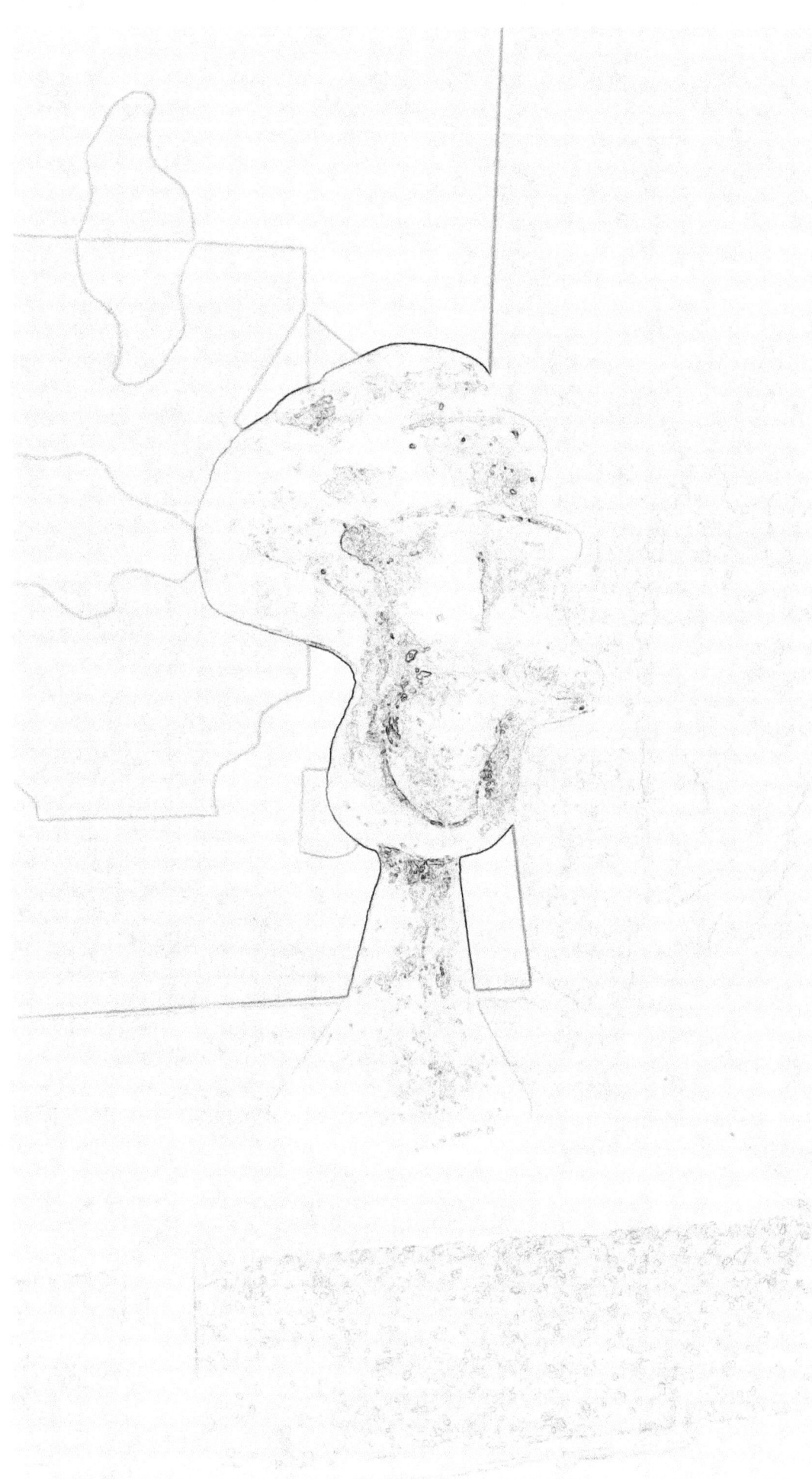